MISSION AMERICA:

D0486640

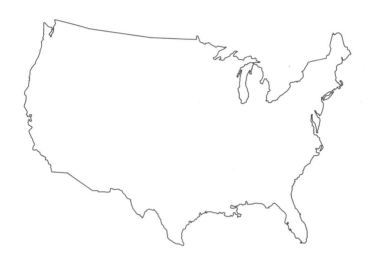

Challenges & Opportunities for Catholics Today

Frank P. DeSiano, CSP

Paulist Press, Mahwah, NJ
www.**paulistpress**.com

Paulist Evangelization Ministries, Washington, DC
www.**pemdc**.org

Cover and book design by Joann Sullivan, Studioworks

ISBN: 978-0-8091-4753-3

Published by Paulist Press, 997 Macarthur Blvd., Mahwah, NJ, 07430-9990
www.paulistpress.com; and
Paulist Evangelization Ministries, 3031 4th St. NE, Washington, DC, 20017
www.pemdc.org.

Printed and bound in the United States of America

May, 2011 Printing

*This book is dedicated to the
memory of many Paulist brothers
who died during its writing, especially
Fr. Frank Diskin, CSP, at 92 years of age,
mature in spirit and joy,
long a mentor to me and many.*

*And to Paulist Fathers
Jim Wiesner,
Jim Moran,
Larry Boadt,
Jim Donovan
all of whom died way too young—
for the companionship they gave us
and the mission they served—
and had yet to serve.*

To any single young man reading this book
who is inspired to give his life in service
to bringing the Gospel as a missionary
to our culture today,
please think about our Paulist mission and way of life.

"Reaching the Unreached in Faith"

Contents

Acknowledgements

There are many people to extend thanks to for their help with this book. The many parishes where I have visited are near the top of the list, and my colleagues at Paulist Evangelization Ministries (formerly, PNCEA), particularly Fr. Kenneth Boyack and Ryan Multer, who read and gave feedback on this material.

Some of the material and ideas in this book appeared previously in different form. I have shared chapter 3 with my Paulist brothers, and some of the ideas in chapter 2 appeared in a very different form as "The Conversion of America: An Exploratory Essay," in *The Catholic Response*, January/February, 2009, vol. V, no. 4, pp. 14–23.

Paulists and pastors, along with diocesan directors of evangelization, also provided helpful perspective: Susan Timoney of Washington, D.C., Fr. John Hurley, CSP, of Baltimore, Diane Kletzak of Tampa, Jeanne Schrempf of Albany, Sr. Louise Alff, OFM of Philadelphia, Deacon Tom Gornick of Portland, Oregon, and Fr. Richard Hynes of Chicago. Paulists John Geaney and Charlie Brunick gave me particular encouragement. Paulist Dat Tran, whose ordination occurs in the year of this book's publication, has inspired many by his commitment to mission.

I am especially grateful for the careful and professional reading given by my Paulist brother Paul Huesing, who provided many helpful suggestions to make my meaning clearer than it was. His thorough readings of the manuscript were invaluable.

His Eminence, Francis Cardinal George, graciously looked at two different versions of this book; his encouragement was a great support to me. The Cardinal has long been deeply committed to mission. The various points where our lives have overlapped have, indeed, been a blessing for me.

I need to especially mention Fr. Jim Donovan, CSP, another Paulist who gave great encouragement and direction, bringing me to expand what I was developing into a more usable pastoral tool. Jim's commitment to mission remained an inspiration to me over five decades. His unexpected death near the end of October 2010 was an enormous shock to all us Paulists.

Penny Mangan, a friend and Paulist Associate from Chicago, provided important contexts for me, along with her nephew Rob Mangan. Their help, particularly with the first several chapters of this book, deserves particular acknowledgement.

Paula Minaert serves as an excellent copy editor for Paulist Evangelization Ministries, and Joann Sullivan as a splendid book designer— my gratitude to them for their help with this book, and all the help they have given our organization over these years.

Denny Marcotte, our business manager, has enormous gifts for getting things done, not least of which was the printing and distribution of this book.

This book is being jointly published by Paulist Press (Mahwah, NJ) and Paulist Evangelization Ministries. I am extremely grateful to Fr. Mark-David Janus, CSP, President of Paulist Press, and his staff, for their cooperation and assistance.

I continue my life-long gratitude to the Paulist Fathers, who have asked me, at this later point in my life, to serve as President of Paulist Evangelization Ministries. My key hope is that this book will further our Paulist vision and substantially increase our sense of mission in the Catholic Church today.

Introduction

Does it make sense to think of America as mission territory?

That depends, in part, on what we think "mission" is. If mission serves primarily to build up Third World and isolated societies in the name of Christ, then the idea of mission to America veers toward the absurd. Yes, there might be, on this reading, explicit missionary areas—urban or rural areas of poverty, some new immigrant groupings or perhaps Native American reservations. But, by and large, America, by definition, is not a Third World society.

If mission, however, means bringing the Gospel to people who have not heard it, or, having heard it, no longer follow it, then America can certainly qualify as mission territory. Indeed, despite a lot of ink spilled over the evangelical revival here of the past three decades, Americans seem to be growing further away from an expressed and explicit faith.

One indicator of this is the American Religious Identity Survey (2008), published in 2009. It shows the number of people who respond "None" to the question about religious affiliation has grown from 9 percent in 1990 to 15 percent in 2008. This number is projected to rise to 25 percent in twenty years. While one may qualify this information with the remark, "But people are more spiritual, even if they attend church less," this presumes that such a distinction can actually survive scrutiny. If spirituality in any way involves commitment, most religious observers would hold that associating with others, i.e., attending a church, synagogue, or mosque, is a basic way to express, and sustain, commitment.

Another indicator might be actual attendance at church on Sunday. Nailing down these figures is notoriously difficult, but the Center for Applied Research in the Apostolate (CARA), located at Georgetown University in Washington, D.C., offers the widest and best sample of Catholic responses. Twenty-three percent of all Catholics claim to attend Mass weekly; another 21 percent claim to attend at least monthly. This means that 56 percent of Catholics do not attend Mass with any regularity; in fact, 32 percent respond that they attend rarely or never. Most of these who don't attend come from younger generations, so Mass attendance is likely to decrease in coming decades.

While Catholics have "held their own" in terms of population growth in the United States, all observers attribute this fact to the growing numbers of Catholics immigrating here. Without this influx of new people, most of whom have Catholic cultural backgrounds, the numbers of Catholics in the United States would have shrunk dramatically. Indeed, some studies have seen an attrition rate of more than 30 percent among Americans raised as Catholics. (One should not presume, further, that Hispanics, having acclimated to the United States, will maintain anything like their present allegiance to Catholicism; they seem quite prone to either drifting from the practice of faith or exploring involvement in non-Catholic congregations.)

It would be honest to note that the categories used in these various surveys might not seem hard and clear to responders. If a Catholic drifts to a non-denominational church for a while, does that mean this person has left the Catholic Church? Even if someone has joined another Christian community as a committed member, this still might not mean in that individual's mind that she or he is no longer a Catholic. Drifting seems to be part of the contemporary Christian scene.

Nevertheless, the basic trends, both within and beyond the Catholic community, track downward. All Catholic pastors and pastoral leaders should have great concern about this. We may be blessed because the oldest generation continues to worship, and suburban churches fill up on Sunday. We would be presumptuous, and blind, to think these numbers will continue into the future. The younger generations of Catholics—indeed of all faiths—have a very different take on participation in formal religion. They will make up the future of all faith traditions in America.

Beyond statistical data, one can point to the broader issue of Catholic identity in American culture. The older paradigm, in which Catholics felt themselves a minority and, as a result, tenaciously held on to their Catholic identity, has given way to a newer paradigm, in which most Catholics feel very much a part of American culture. This complicates Catholic identity enormously. Catholics seem to be growing in their tolerance of certain state-permitted practices that are clearly prohibited by Catholic teaching. While abortion and same-sex marriage stand out most egregiously, this trend has long been growing as American culture has become more secular. We only have to think of how society, in the past fifty years, has changed in terms of acceptance of divorce, sexual activity outside marriage, and contraception.

Catholic leaders want to at least hold the line in terms of legally-permitted limits; in some cases, like abortion, they want to actually change civil law. Many Catholics, however, give the impression that such a line is not worth fighting as hard for in the cultural arena. In another arena, whatever might be officially propounded in terms of social justice, just war, or immigration policy, Catholics appear to divide on these issues according to party lines and individual circumstances. Catholics today seem quite willing to accept pluralism in moral practice.

As a result, Catholics do not stand apart as much as they used to. This preoccupies Catholic leaders who, rightly, fear a loss of Catholic identity. It should cause even greater fear among European bishops, who have seen not only Catholic, but Christian identity itself, almost vanish from the public sphere (not to mention its elimination in much of private life).

But just shoring up Catholic identity, as necessary as that may be, hardly does justice to the Catholic mission in America. In fact, it may be precisely a lack of a strong mission impulse toward seekers and people of marginal religious practice that, in some way, is causing a slippage in Catholic identity. As long as Catholics spend most of their energy internally, trying to push one or another emphasis, instead of powerfully and compellingly inviting people to consider what the Catholic faith can offer them, we are acting with something less than the essential components of our Catholic message. Catholics cannot erase the dynamics of mission from our vision. Doing so has consequences for people both inside and outside the Church.

I believe that Catholics have to learn anew how rich, important, and essential is the message that they bring to people today: rich in its tradition and lived expression, important for God's purpose in the world, and essential for understanding how much Catholics offer today's world. As long as Catholics cannot state compellingly why someone should become a Catholic, or why it is dynamically important for them to invite people to Catholicism, we cannot, by that same token, give a coherent picture of our own faith even to ourselves. To actually share faith is the best way to reinforce it in the believer.

The de facto dominance of a Protestant evangelical cast to the contemporary discussion of faith creates a major challenge to, and opportunity for, the way Catholics look at, and present, themselves. It is not just a matter of speaking more clearly to our own people, our captive audience, if you will; it is much more a matter of learning how to speak more powerfully and compellingly to an ever more elusive world.

In this book—directed at pastors, pastoral associates, adult faith directors, and parish leaders—I try to address some of these questions. I start by looking at issues of conversion in the hearts of people, particularly as the current American religious sentiment frames the issue. The second chapter broadens the scope, to reflect on some of the societal issues of conversion—what does it mean to bring the Gospel to America? Giving full due to ecumenical and interfaith efforts, I believe that without a sweeping affirmation of what it has to offer people today, and of the call to share faith, Catholicism inevitably grows lethargic.

This leads to an important issue for Catholics and all believers, which is treated in chapter 3: how do we describe the impulse for mission today? If we have become, in effect, mostly universalists, believing that most people are saved, what implications does this have for our own sense of having something to give to people today? Do we not need to review and critically edit some of our assumptions about salvation in order to do justice to the very issues human life raises?

This leads to a look at the context for mission in America in chapter 4. Religion in today's America has taken on a definite evangelical form. Does the basic approach to faith in the United States have anything to tell us Catholics? After identifying five elements that describe this form of "American religion," I raise the question: what does this mean in terms of our American parishes? Is there a way that parishes in America are called to be, simply because we *are* in America in the early decades of the twenty-first century? A fifth chapter sketches some outlines of what faith will look like in the future, even for us Catholics, given the dynamics in society today.

These reflections lead me to the object of this book, in chapter 6: to sketch an agenda for today's American parish, primarily as a way to help parishes think more clearly about what they are doing, where their priorities are, and why. Some readers need to skip to the end of a book— if that is your profile, I invite you to skip to chapter 6 at any time. The first five chapters fill in some of the background to what I present as a contemporary agenda for parishes. Finally, an overview of a New Testament missionary spirituality, presented as an appendix, finishes these reflections.

These essays are all an attempt to help our American parishes retrieve their missionary energy. Since every parish shares in the bishop's apostolic mandate, every parish should be a community of apostles. Canon 528 lays out the rudiments of a missionary vision of parish, explicitly naming outreach to inactive Catholics and to seekers as part of a pastor's agenda. There is sufficient evidence to believe that our sense of mission was much greater decades ago—and to worry that it has significantly contracted since then.

Back in 1950, when there were twenty-seven and a half million Catholics, we received a little more than 119,000 adults into the Church (a ratio of .43 percent). In 1960, almost forty-one million Catholics welcomed about 140,000 people into the Church (a ratio of .36 percent). By 1970, almost forty-eight million Catholics received only 92,000 adults into the Church (a ratio of .19 percent). By 1980, the ratio had dropped to .16 percent, with fifty million Catholics receiving 82,000 adult converts. By the turn of the millennium this ratio had risen to .28 percent (sixty-two million Catholics receiving 171,000 adults); but in 2009, the ratio had dropped again to .18 percent, with sixty-eight million Catholics receiving 124,000 converts. The 2010 directory lists only 119,000 adults received into the Church. In other words, sixty-eight million Catholics received the same number of adults into the Church as twenty-eight million did sixty years before.

A chart makes the situation more graphic:

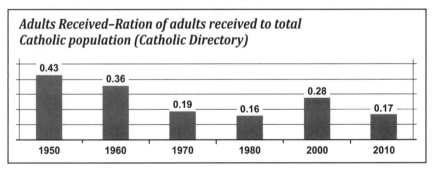

Adults Received–Ration of adults received to total Catholic population (Catholic Directory)

1950	1960	1970	1980	2000	2010
0.43	0.36	0.19	0.16	0.28	0.17

In short, the numbers of converts (for comparison sake, this number includes those adults baptized into the Catholic Church and those received into full communion) has, proportionally, dropped by half over the past sixty years. (Catholics often do not realize that from 1950 to 1980 a high birth rate accounted for growth. Since then, growth has been mostly from immigration.) One might, with justification, point to many factors that influence these varying percentages—ecumenical and marital trends, for example. I think, however, it would be very hard to discount the simple dissipation of our missionary zeal—our burning desire to bring what we have, in all its profundity, to a society that would, on many levels, certainly benefit from receiving our Catholic message, as I try to show in chapter 2.

If parishes in America can recover a missionary spirit, perhaps it might spill over into other parts of the world, notably Europe. After all, as we will see in chapter 2, America's engagement with religion is really religion's engagement with modernity. Modernity, at least in the form of its legacy from the Enlightenment, thrives more fully in Europe than in the United States. If religion in America can make some headway in addressing modernity, this may be of particular help to Europe; it may forestall, too, a similar downturn when Latin America starts to deal with modernity in earnest. The world, for better or worse, pays attention to American trends.

I hope this little book produces "chatter"—conversation among our-selves as Catholic leaders and, therefore, as Catholic apostles. I believe we can, without setting aside any advance in ecumenical or interfaith insights, powerfully upgrade our outreach to seekers and those who have no active faith community. In another book (*Why Not Consider Becoming a Catholic?*, PNCEA, 2010, *www.pncea.org*) I tried to lay out the apologetic foundation for mission—that we Catholics have an essential message to offer people today. In this book, I try to lay out the theoretical and practical pieces of this mission. If either of these efforts spurs people forward, then a little part of my obligations as an American missionary, a Paulist, will have been fulfilled.

Chapter 1

Conversion of People

"I've only got two this year."

"I've got six, but it's early yet. One or two more will show up by December."

I hear these kinds of statements in the fall each year as I go around parishes. Directors of Religious Education or Adult Faith Formation recount the numbers of people who have emerged to be part of their R.C.I.A. While some of these will become catechumens, most will inevitably be candidates; that is, most of the people who come forward already are part of a Christian religious tradition. While they might think of themselves as converts, Catholic vocabulary at the moment does not describe them with that word. Candidates are considered already believers in some basic way; in the R.C.I.A., they are primarily completing their initiation in the Catholic Church.

Catechumens, however, are considered converts, people moving from a state of being unbaptized to one in which they will be fully initiated into the Church by the three basic sacraments that mark full membership as a Catholic Christian. The fundamental process of the Rite of Christian Initiation of Adults (R.C.I.A.), promulgated in the years after the Second Vatican Council in the 1970s, applies in situations as different as non-Christian Africa and downtown Rome. It brings people through a process of inquiry, from the stage of catechumens (if they are unbaptized), to that of elect (if they choose to be baptized), to that of neophyte once they are baptized. Specific rites accompany the latter stages of being elect, notably the Scrutinies during the time of Lent. After Baptism, they complete the rites by going through a period of mystagogy, that is, more intense learning about Christian life.

Two fundamental dramas take place under the rubric of conversion. One involves what we think conversion is. The other entails our fundamental approach, as Catholics, to conversion: whether we think seeking conversion is something we actively pursue, or whether we see ourselves basically blessing what has already happened in someone's life. From the statistics presented in the introduction, my impression is that the impetus to call people to conversion is getting weaker and, given present trends, will only get even weaker in the future.

This chapter will look at the first issue, the idea of conversion itself as it applies to individuals. Chapter 2 will look at why, in today's culture, we do or do not put energy into the process of inviting people to the Catholic faith.

The Background Buzz

Discussion of conversion today entails the wider phenomenon of Christian faith in America today, the movement of the American mind from mainstream Protestant churches to the evangelical/non-denominational congregations that appear to garner most of the comment in media circles today.

Of course, all discussion of conversion is painted with the even broader phenomenon of secularity, of a gradual diminishment of the role of religion in today's secular state and, even more, of the demise of a sense of the divine, of fundamental religious assumptions. This has been well documented. Full-fledged atheists command attention on our radio shows and in bookstores, urging people to give up the illusions which, they claim, come with a belief that they attribute to childishness and fear. Likewise, recent surveys show the astonishing rise in the numbers of people who will answer "None" when asked their religious preference.

Against this background of growing secularity stands the seemingly growing reality of an evangelical Christianity that challenges the fundamental way Christians have passed on their faith: infant baptism. Since at least the time of St. Augustine, Christians have baptized their children, presuming and creating a link between one generation and another. In pre-medieval and medieval times, as certain tribes became Christian, they assumed this passing on of faith within their cultures. Even after the Protestant Reformation, with the exception of certain Protestant groups like the Anabaptists, many people used Baptism to pass on religious identity to their children—the Irish baptizing their children as Catholics, the Danes as Lutherans, the Scots as Presbyterians.

One can pose a fundamental question about this process in these words: were people raised this way, over the past 1600 years and more, really converted? Were they believers? Or was this mostly just some kind of external, social process without true inner change? Were they, as so many Catholics put it, catechized but not evangelized? Another way to put this can be: is Christian life defined solely having a personal relationship with Jesus, with Jesus as one's "personal Lord and Savior," as this is put in an evangelical framework? Is anything else inadequate? For Catholics, all of this raises basic questions about conversion.

What is Christian conversion?

Defining conversion does not come easily. Christians have lived through very different epochs and experienced a variety of situations in life; conversion has different nuances as a result. To convert as an adult in the first century surely meant something different than a twenty-first century Christian moving from one Christian congregation to another. To experience conversion as a member of a group, as happened during the Christian expansion among the tribes in the Roman Empire, would carry one set of meanings; to enter the Catholic Church as a former Jew or Muslim would mean something very different, whether in Medieval times or today.

Do we get any help by looking at what the word meant in New Testament writings? The Greek verb *metanoiein* is usually translated as "repent," in the sense of turning away from something. However, this word carries for modern people overtones of "penance" or "doing penance," whereas the root of the verb in Greek talks about "turning one's mind around." In the Gospel according to Mark, where this word has a prominent place in the initial teaching of Jesus, just sixteen verses from the very first verse, we read: "After the handing over of John the Baptist, Jesus went into Galilee proclaiming the Good News (=Gospel) of God. And he said, 'The special time has been fulfilled and the Kingdom of God has come near; turn your mind around and believe in the Good News'" (my translation).

Jesus, then, comes proclaiming God's Good News; that news is specified by the fulfillment of God's special, appointed time, God's special moment; the Kingdom of God has come near. Conversion, then, seems directly related to God's Good News, to the drawing near of the Kingdom of God. The change of mind to which Jesus calls people involves seeing and accepting this special time of grace, which Jesus calls the *Kingdom*.

John the Baptist came before Jesus, proclaiming a "baptism of repentance (conversion) for the forgiveness of sins." Jesus' proclamation contains, for sure, John's message, but it goes much beyond that; it points to a readiness to accept the Kingdom of God. In case anyone has questions about what the Kingdom implies, Mark's subsequent verses in chapters 2 and 3 show the implications of the Kingdom in Jesus' healing, forgiveness, exorcism, and preaching.

Conversion, then, means (for adults, at least) a readiness to accept God's Good News, inaugurated by Jesus. In view of Jesus' life, it now contains both the announcement of God's special time and its founding in the death and resurrection of Jesus. This is why the beginning of the Gospel according to Mark, announces the *Good News of Jesus Christ*. It is Jesus' message about the Kingdom, but now fulfilled, in his life, teaching, death, and resurrection.

Modern Protestant Evangelical Ideas

Modern evangelicals, who have transformed the landscape of our discussion about conversion, have phrased conversion as "accepting Jesus as one's personal Lord and Savior." They generally locate conversion as an emotional experience. It is not clear, that is, that someone can just *say*, "I accept Jesus as my personal Lord and Savior," as a verbal formula. Rather, the phrase presumes something has been going on inside the person emotionally and consciously.

There is not a Catholic, or even mainline Protestant, who has not been affected by this way of putting the question. Sincere evangelicals approach Catholics, Episcopalians, Methodists, and other mainline believers, asking if they have really accepted Jesus as their personal Lord and Savior. I, a Catholic priest, have been approached by evangelical Protestants and even some charismatic Catholics, with the question: "Have I really accepted Jesus; is my relationship with him truly personal?" Obviously, the total commitment of my life to following Jesus does not seem sufficient for some of these folks.

As the evangelical formula is generally elaborated, "accepting Jesus as my personal Savior" forms a definitive moment of salvation: evangelicals identify a specific moment when "salvation" happens. A further elaboration of this formula goes on to assert that, once saved, a personal cannot be unsaved; that is, salvation is final and definitive, even if one should later commit serious sin. One day on a transcontinental flight I overheard a conversation between two people across the aisle proceeding exactly along these lines.

This is the basis on which many people who define themselves as Christian will dismiss the religious experience of many other Christians, because these churches do not have a requirement about a particular emotional experience as a requisite for salvation or membership in a church. Or because the formula about Jesus as one's personal Lord and Savior has not been used. Obviously most of these mainline churches (Catholic, Protestant, and Orthodox) baptize infants who lack the maturity to formulate much, let alone make some kind of decision about Jesus. This element of infant baptism sharply differentiates mainline churches from evangelicals, as I am using the word. In non-evangelical churches, children can be baptized because of their identity with a community (generally through the family) and be deemed among the potentially saved. In evangelical terms, salvation has to happen through individual decision. To be sure, evangelicals might make other accommodations to keep from feeling that their unbaptized children are damned, but these would be the exception that proves the rule. In place of Baptism, for example, the child is dedicated to God.

One of the major ways evangelicals outline the pattern of conversion is through some determination of stress, with a subsequent relief from that stress through the message of salvation. So people adjudge themselves as sinners, as addicts, as reprobate, or as unsaved in other ways. Then, through assent to Jesus Christ, or his Spirit, they experience a relief, a liberation, from what bound them or filled them with guilt or shame. Perhaps no other hymn reveals this pattern as much as the old favorite, "Amazing Grace." "How sweet the sound that saved a wretch like me. . . . I once was lost but now am found, was blind but now I see." This kind of experience certainly a has strong place in all Christian life.

The gist of this pattern was identified fairly well by William James in his famous book, *The Varieties of Religious Experience*. His category of "twice born," which he distinguished from the category of "once born," captured the essence of the conversion experience as he defined it: a sense of a bad and shameful past life, followed by an experience involving religious language, and then a different subsequent sense of being "saved," or "reborn." Interestingly, James thought a transition like this could happen in a variety of even non-religious ways (through counseling, for example); when it happened through religious experience, however, he called it conversion. The "once born," which he generally, and somewhat incorrectly, identified with Catholics, did not have this experience of disruption in life; the "once born" had no past that felt enormously bad or shameful.

Biblical Issues

When one considers the broad strokes of biblical and Christian experience, one might well wonder if the American evangelical's account of conversion does justice to the actual reality of conversion. One does not, for example, find a clear "before" and "after" in the lives of most of the Apostles and other followers of Jesus, in the sense of stress or shame turning into a moment of liberation. One might point to the experience of Easter as a clear "before/after" in the case of the Twelve; that certainly was decisive, but not as an experience from brokenness to wholeness (excepting, perhaps, Peter). Likewise, one might point to Pentecost, but that experience was more a movement from fear of persecution to bold proclamation.

Mary Magdalene surely shows the "twice born" pattern, but many of the other women who followed Jesus do not. One does not see any of this in the image of Mary, the mother of Jesus; indeed, for Luke and Matthew, Mary was in some way always chosen and blessed. Nor does one see this in the initial conversions as narrated in Acts 2; the three thousand people who join the Church do so because they accept a message, not because they have a powerful emotional experience. That they were "cut to the heart," as the NRSV translates it, hardly demands a modern, histrionic reading. Similarly, all those who, *along with their households*, accept conversion, do so because of the message of salvation (e.g., Acts 11:14; 16:34). Parents and masters brought their children and slaves into the Christian experience; conversion was collective, and not just in the individualized, personal form of modern evangelical Christianity.

The message of salvation certainly contained more than information or bland doctrinal formulas. But neither is it laden with a lot of "inner-turmoil" content. The message had a dramatic effect on peoples' lives primarily because of the role it played in the eschatological pattern that shaped the consciousness of first-century believers. This eschatological background seems to have been effective in both Jewish and Gentile circles, though it obviously played out differently in each group. Peter's speech in Acts 2 differs substantially from Paul's speech to the Athenians in Acts 17—granting that Luke is not giving us anything like a tape-recorded representation in either account. Peter can appeal to a coming judgment based on Jewish tradition, a judgment tied to Luke's whole approach to prophets who must die in Jerusalem (Jesus being the prime instance of this). Paul, on the other hand, appeals to Greek poets and a much more general sense of God's impending decision to judge human-kind. "While God has overlooked the times of human ignorance, now he commands all people everywhere to repent, because he has fixed a day on which he will have the world judged in righteousness by a man whom he has appointed. . ." (Acts 17:30-31).

Christians in the first century, then, became believers because they wanted to insert themselves into the larger pattern that Jesus had opened for them. Undoubtedly, some of these believers had strong psychological motives and large troves of shame. Just as surely, however, most of these believers saw an overall pattern of God establishing something new in the world (a new people, a new covenant, a new option) and wanted to identify themselves with this new pattern, with Jesus and what he represented. People, whether Jewish or Gentile, saw in Jesus an alternative to their lives. Paul's arguments about this in the early chapters of Romans speak as much to the total situation of humans, whether Jewish or Gentile, as to any psychological trauma. Even the famous "internal debate" of Romans 7 ("that which I will, I do not"), though often interpreted as some kind of personal, existential anguish on Paul's part, is likely Paul's way of characterizing the limits to accessing God, which Jesus now has transcended in his resurrection by the bestowal of his Spirit.

Furthermore, while some Christians readily construe these early conversions as full and final, there is plenty of evidence in the New Testament that, even after conversion, early Christians continued to sin. Conversion was hardly the final step for them. They still had to persevere, to be faithful. It is hard to explain the sections of exhortation in almost all of Paul's letters, his consistent warnings (particularly in 1 Corinthians 10), if the members of his congregations had everything in order. Likewise, many of the parables of Jesus make no sense if Christianity is a "done deal" from the moment of conversion, as we will see below.

Questions for Evangelicals

The primarily "emotional stress/personal relief" description of conversion that evangelical Americans broadly assume (an assumption growing to some extent even in mainline Protestant and Catholic communities) has some troubling, if not distorted, dimensions to it. Acknowledging these difficulties, and finding a better way to express the experience of conversion, might help clarify issues of conversion all the way around, for evangelicals and for all Christians. Let's look at some of these difficulties.

One downside of the modern evangelical approach is this: what if people do not feel strong psychological movements in themselves? What if they do not feel stress or anxiety? What if they are not overwhelmed by a sense of sin or shame? What if their lives are not dysfunctional or destructive? Might there still not be a desire to become a follower of Jesus, even absent these internal, psychological forces? Is it not far better to recognize the many ways people have come, and do come, to faith, than to restrict faith to primarily stressful feelings?

Next, at what point does someone set his or her mind and heart on conversion? When has one made a definitive decision? Evangelical churches have to constantly deal with the issue of backsliding, a problem recognized in the early Church and present in all of church history. The parable of the Sower and the Seed (leading the collection of parables in Matthew 13 and Mark 4) shows that the problems people had in persevering in the faith existed from the days of the early Church. Evangelicals, then, can appear to identify a moment of conversion as being far more decisive than it actually is. The New Testament is always concerned with people remaining faithful.

This dovetails with yet a third downside of the modern evangelical approach to Christianity: the impression that conversion is virtually identical to salvation, that the moment of conversion has overtones of the *eschaton*, of the final days. Evangelicals garner from various half-threads in the New Testament the impression that once salvation has been given, it can never be taken away and, further, that salvation is given with the moment of conversion. "I *have been* saved" is the phrase, not, "I am on the road to salvation."

A fourth difficulty is the need, in the evangelical approach, to return to the psychological moment of relief again and again, as if this were the ultimate pattern of Christian experience. How can one, with this view, escape the ongoing labor of proving to oneself yet once again that one has accepted Jesus, that one has been freed, and that one needs to have joy and prosperity (or whatever) as a sign of one's salvation? How can people be certain, over time, that they have truly converted? The very frailty of human emotional states plays against the wisdom of putting Christian experience into this kind of framework. Does this not almost require preaching primarily around conversion, and worship primarily replicating the "moment of conversion"? I remember visiting one evangelical church and noting, in amazement, the boxes of Kleenex tissue placed between every seat in the congregation.

A fifth problem comes with the black-and-white approach to the issue of salvation. Only those who know they are saved can be saved, according to this formula. Therefore, the presumption moves to the non-salvation of all those who have not gone through the psychological formula that evangelicals put forward as the criterion of faith. The world, then, is divided into those who know they are saved, and the rest who are not saved. This is, on its face, a direct contradiction of the parable of judgment in Matthew 25, where people are saved *in spite of their not knowing* who they helped, and how it happened that they have come to have a place in the Kingdom.

The evangelical construal of conversion properly challenges the automatic passing on of faith through purely cultural means—cultural forms that have led to widespread nominal Christianity in the United States and, even more, Europe. It should be raising questions about the meaning of conversion. Conversion, and Christian faith, should not be nominal. But the evangelical construal cannot be a total answer to what Christians mean by conversion. As we have seen, it causes too many issues to arise because of the way it sees religious experience. Is there a better way to ground the issue of conversion?

A Sturdier Grounding

How do we avoid the notion of seeing conversion primarily as feeling, of trauma-being-relieved, but still allow the importance of various feelings in the process? How can our thinking permit a range of Christian experience, even the unfortunate and tragic experience of sin after conversion? There is another way to think of conversion, one open to most of Christian experience over the centuries, one that can take account of the phenomenon of ongoing and deeper involvement in the mystery of Jesus, one that people can grow into, and one more firmly grounded in Scripture.

I believe that thinking of conversion *as identifying with Christ* can possibly ground Christian thinking more securely in Scripture and also in Christian experience.

Before pointing out the advantages of this approach, I must address the situation of children because much conversion language calls for behaviors that children, obviously, cannot fulfill. How do children make acts of faith, trust, acceptance of Jesus, rejection of sin, and other such signs of conversion? They cannot, of course, in themselves.

However, a broader, more encompassing, sense of community has always been part of Christian experience—the sense that a believing core carries along those who are on the edge. Notice how St. Paul puts it in 1 Corinthians 7:14: "For the unbelieving husband is made holy through his wife, and the unbelieving wife is made holy through her husband. Otherwise, your children would be unclean, but as it is, they are holy." Paul obviously has some kind of collective notion of community whereby nonbelievers connected to the community are in some way affected by it. Conversion had, for him, communal dimensions. This is a way to think of children—they are connected to the community of faith and, because of that, they participate in the faith of believers. In some sense, these collective ideas of conversion and belonging to Jesus have created nuanced ways of thinking about conversion and salvation.

What, then, grounds the experience of conversion for adults? While modern society has a harder and harder time with adulthood—when does one become an adult? Later and later it seems!—adult conversion has become the norm of reflection for Catholics. So what is the heart of conversion, in adults and, by extension, in non-adults or those not able to have a sound mind? My suggestion would be: *a set of decisions, arising from a variety of human situations, to identify with Jesus Christ as the result of God's free gift. Such a decision would carry two distinct vectors: absolute trust in God and a total commitment to (theological) love.*

Such a set of decisions, in adults, may or may not have a strong emotional component. They may be more decisive at one point in life than in another. They may not point to any one particular moment. Rather, they likely point to an unfolding direction in life. They are, unfortunately, reversible. They may come in a primarily personal framework, but they may arise, too, from a primarily cultural context. People may, and often do, grow into this set of decisions, beginning in childhood. These decisions shape the Christian life in different ways, as the meaning of Jesus and his teaching (and his community) impact believers' lives over time.

Unpacking Some of These Elements

Adult conversion, obviously, is an experience for people once they reach a relatively mature consciousness. The experience can have multiple forms and levels of human emotional expression, but, at the very least, it is a conscious decision to see God, as revealed in Jesus and the Spirit, at the center of one's life. For some, it certainly can be an experience of total breakdown and restoration. For others, it can be a quest for completion. For some, it might come as an expression of belonging to a universal community, or as a move toward universal compassion. For others, it might reveal itself as part of the search for beauty or truth.

However experienced, it results from grace, from the free and abundant love of God shown in Jesus Christ and poured out through the Spirit of Jesus. Even though people may employ specific actions on their way to conversion (prayer, searching the Scriptures, talking with friends, cleaning up messy parts in life), conversion is impossible outside the framework of grace. This grace of God forms an enveloping horizon for people. It may be concretely experienced in particular ways (a sudden insight, the gift of tears) more or less clear to the person; or it may not be expressed so powerfully. However it is expressed, the horizon of grace is absolute. One identifies with Jesus because God has identified with humankind in Jesus Christ.

In response to grace (that reality of God's overwhelming love shown in Jesus and made present through the Spirit), people make a choice (the choice itself is a further instance of grace). What is the nature of that choice? One way or another, it entails putting God, as revealed by Jesus, ahead of everything else in life. Jesus indicated this direction with his injunction, expressed in various ways in the New Testament, that people had to take up their cross, had to "hate" all relations, if they would be his disciples (e.g., Luke 14:26-27).

For a Christian, putting God at the center means identifying with Jesus Christ through the Holy Spirit. Christ becomes such a focus of a person's vision that they see, sense, affirm, and respond to God as Jesus did. Christ becomes such a point of identity for the convert that they experience unity with his death and resurrection. Paul expresses this in a variety of ways in his writings. For example, he puts it powerfully in Galatians 2:19-20: "I have been crucified with Christ; and it is no longer I who live, but it is Christ who lives in me." And, at the end of the same letter (6:17): ". . . for I carry the marks of Jesus branded on my body." Just as starkly, we can read Paul in Philippians (3:10-11): "I want to know Christ and the power of his resurrection and the sharing of his sufferings by becoming like him in his death, if somehow I may attain the resurrection from the dead."

One notes here the fundamental framework of Christian existence, the pattern of death and resurrection (a pattern explored more fully in the appendix). Expressed on a variety of levels (personal, sacramental, moral), a decision to follow Christ means enacting his death and resurrection in various ways in one's own life. Paul clearly reveals this in his discussion of baptism in Romans 6, where he primarily is talking about a change in moral direction (Romans 6:11-12). All the gospel statements about the cost of discipleship point to the need to accept one's cross and renounce what does not belong to the Kingdom of God.

If, through grace, believers decide to make God the center of their lives by identifying with Jesus Christ, then, clearly, the commitments of Jesus become those of the convert. There are both internal and external aspects to this commitment, but they all relate to the central theme of the life of Jesus, the Kingdom of God. The Sermon on the Mount, the parables, the wondrous deeds of Jesus, his death and resurrection, all centered on that for which he lived, the Kingdom of God. To identify with Jesus means grasping a new and deeper relationship with God in such a way that it transforms our relationships with others.

The basic internal commitment is *absolute trust in God*. Jesus shows us this in the Sermon on the Mount and its cognate passages: why need we worry about what we will eat or drink? If God cares for even the grass and the birds, as God obviously and beautifully does, then will not God care for us as well? Matthew 6:24 ff. sketches the kind of trust that followers of Jesus should have. Even more, Jesus shows this in his attitude toward the death he would accept as part of bringing the Kingdom to fullness. Luke sketches Jesus as the greatest of the prophets, all of whom must die in Jerusalem, for "it is impossible for a prophet to die outside of Jerusalem" (Luke 13:33).

Such unconditional trust does not come easily, even to those who have undergone conversion, because of the radical shift it demands in a person's life. The impulses attributed to our archetypical first parents in Eden remain very strong in all of us. We all want to guarantee our own security, control our own lives, dictate the boundaries of our own existence, and pretend that we are in control. We all hesitate to fully accept Jesus' point that every hair in our head is known by God (Luke 21:18).

The basic external commitment expresses itself in *theological love.* The word "theological" distinguishes between the love arising in conversion from the general emotional blur that Americans associate with love. Often modern people, when they talk of love, refer to the feelings that arise inside because of some attraction. Theological love receives its motivation from the being of God, manifested as faithful and enduring love in the Hebrew Scriptures, and as "charity" in the Christian Scriptures. (Unfortunately, the word "charity" has taken on very patronizing connotations, even despite Pope Benedict's attempt to rescue the word.) Theological love puts others at the center, not one's self.

Theological love arises primarily from concern for the other. Theological love calls for identifying with others (as Jesus himself identified with others), particularly those excluded by conventional social systems. As Jesus lived for the poor, the sinner, the despairing, the confused, the seeking, and the physically limited, so conversion to Christ calls for the same kind of generous living. Theological love also calls for some kind of explicit life in community, with other believers, as disciples support one another and manifest their faith in prayer and sacrament.

Conversion to Jesus, then, means conversion to his Kingdom, with its double manifestation of absolute trust and theological love. It involves a discipleship that inherently connects with others in two ways: it serves others in humility and it relies on others for its growth and support. Church experience hardly contradicts this authentic conversion. The diminishment of loyalty that American evangelicalism has generated as it has moved believers to travel from one church expression to another (calling this conversion!) may inadvertently be leading to the inability of modern people to connect with any church expression. Church has become relative, or, worse, irrelevant. Ultimately this leaves people unconnected and, therefore, unsupported in their conversion and discipleship. Inasmuch as all the writings of the New Testament are church documents, modern evangelical takes on personal (emphasizing non-church) conversion deviate profoundly from New Testament experience. Church is not some convenient add-on to conversion, but its very context, its fertile soil.

Thinking of conversion as identifying with Christ has one great consequence: one can recognize analogues of this conversion in the lives even of people who are not conscious believers. They may begin to live for the values of the Kingdom in some implicit ways in their lives. They can grow incrementally in their identification with Jesus. They may well have some sense of openness to God, of acknowledging the power and presence of God, and identifying with the basic elements of the cause of Jesus, the Kingdom. To live for others, to be willing to put to death the sinful conditions of their lives, to trust unconditionally in God, to see patterns of death and resurrection—these, obviously, can happen with God's grace even in the lives of those who do not call themselves Christians. While they may not be defined as converted, they may well be acknowledged as "not far from the Kingdom of God," to use a formula of Jesus (Mark 12:34). They may have, then, some implicit identity with Jesus Christ, even without explicitly knowing about him.

Implications

So how do evangelical patterns challenge the traditionally accepted patterns of transmitting faith? What does it mean to convert? Can Catholics come to think of themselves as converted? Is faith among Catholics often only nominal?

Catholic priests and pastoral associates deal with this on a regular basis. Parents, often non-practicing and sometimes even unmarried, bring children in for Baptism. What can it mean to baptize that child? Is conversion some automatic inoculation that comes through pouring water? Priests, deacons, and lay leaders have challenged Catholic parents to use this moment to re-identify themselves with Jesus Christ. As they wish Christ's life for their children, how can this happen unless they live Christ's life themselves in some explicit way?

For Catholics and mainline Protestants, therefore, evangelical patterns clearly mean that conversion cannot be a side issue. It is not something that comes with one's ethnic background or with simply identifying oneself as a Catholic anymore. The Archdiocese of Chicago has noted that for every one hundred children baptized, only half will receive Confirmation; of those receiving Confirmation, only half will marry in the Church. Catholic schools, with the attendant Catholic culture that developed between 1870 and 1950, are under enormous stress. Catholic schools, which once seemed a permanent fixture, now are closing in dioceses across the country. We are slowly evolving other means of passing on faith.

Faith will be transmitted only if it is seen as the product of grace and conscious, consistent choice on the part of believers. Faith can no longer come in *primarily* institutional and organizational patterns; it has to come in relational patterns as well. While evangelical accounts of conversion have their difficulties, they do throw down the gauntlet for every Christian believer, Catholic and other: have we, at our core, identified our lives with Jesus Christ? Have the patterns of death and resurrection been acknowledged and accepted in the lives of believers? Do the sacraments believers receive reflect authentic transformation in their lives? Does a life of faith receive support from communal and personal patterns of behavior? Is faith consistently expressed in prayer and worship?

The R.C.I.A. does give guidance in this to Catholics—it shows the fruit of adult conversion and, therefore, what conversion should look like, eventually, for every believer. While being raised in a faith seems radically different from accepting a faith as an adult, both point to one supreme goal: discipleship in Jesus Christ, conscious and growing in adults, implicit and incipient in children and teens. Catechetical efforts have just begun to identify other modes of formation apart from the classroom approach used in both Catholic schools and catechetical programs for youth. Intergenerational groups, in which adults and children share the Gospel together, may not solve the whole issue, but they begin to solve some of them.

Sometimes we are tempted to think that Catholics are basically unconverted. We take up the same assumptions of evangelical Christianity, that an explicit, adult, felt experience has to happen for conversion to be real. Certainly, many Catholics who have made a Cursillo or gone through the Life in the Spirit Seminar would point to an experience like this. On the other hand, sometimes we may be tempted to presume that Catholics are converted just because they have been baptized as Catholics.

Seeing conversion as radical identification with Jesus Christ shows a more nuanced picture. In one sense, as Pope Paul VI pointed out in *On*

Evangelization in the Modern World, all of us need deeper evangelization because none of us has fully identified with Jesus, or fully responded to his Spirit. On the other hand, identifying with Jesus Christ can take many forms, sometimes forms that are not explicit or explicitly felt. People, after all, can grow up in an environment of conversion. They are acted upon by others who, through God's grace, live humble lives of service, trust, love, and devotion.

So a clear goal for Catholic leaders, preachers, and pastoral directors arises from today's American environment of conversion: how to help Catholics appropriate more consciously and explicitly the conversion—the identifying with Jesus—that has begun in their lives. Leaders today need to figure out more clearly how we invite Catholics to build upon the seminal experiences of faith that come from family and community. We have to help people grow into discipleship. We have to help Catholics understand themselves as disciples. Pastoral leaders, by using more relational language, can help Catholics clarify the conversion that is ongoing in their lives. Chapter 6 will elaborate how parishes can better emphasize elements of discipleship for Catholics today.

The drama of conversion will not go away. Documents from Rome have stressed more and more the commitment side of Catholic formation. They talk about a *personal adherence* to the person of Jesus, a hanging onto him, as the fulcrum of Christian life. Modern life, with its new patterns of growing up, which we will see in chapter 5, makes the issue of conversion pressing because these patterns call people to choose again and again the key identity of their lives. These new patterns of maturing demand the structures of discipleship.

When Pope Paul insisted that evangelization is the very essence of the Church, he could just as well have said that, in some respects, conversion is the basic business of Catholics. This is not conversion in its somewhat traumatized American version, or conversion as virtually full sanctification, but conversion in its fundamental meaning of having our minds transformed because we have come to identify, as we go through the stages of our lives, again and again with Jesus Christ, and, as a result, to live for his Kingdom.

Questions

1. What do you see as the heart of conversion? What kinds of people would you describe as converted to Jesus? Do you think conversion is a rare event or something quite common?

2. What do you make of the view of conversion as "accepting Jesus Christ as my personal Lord and Savior"? What positive, and negative, points does this view raise for Christians who baptize their children?

3. What do you think would nurture the sense of conversion in Catholics today? What assets do we have as a Church that you think particularly further conversion—such as liturgy, Scripture, spiritual traditions, and so forth? Which assets do you think speak most clearly to Catholics today? How can the Mass more clearly emphasize conversion?

Chapter 2

Conversion in American Society

"We've only got two this year for the R.C.I.A."

Here is another phrase I sometimes hear in the fall, as catechumenal directors are gathering groups that will spend the better part of a year—and sometimes longer than a year—grappling with the Gospel and God's personal call in their lives as they participate in the formal process of conversion that we call the Rite of Christian Initiation of Adults. And what might pastoral leaders mean when they speak this way?

- Perhaps the phrase acknowledges that conversion is God's gift, not the dictate of believers, and we rejoice that God has given this gift to at least two people.

- Perhaps it acknowledges a similar truth: that conversion is not about numbers—which is difficult for us results-oriented modern people to accept.

- Perhaps, more pointedly, it also is a way of saying that we did not invite others to the catecumenate very cogently, that we kept our invitations fairly limited; and our insipid efforts resulted in having only two people.

Let's face it: "insipid" often well describes our efforts. In most parishes, invitation to the process of conversion gets airtime mostly in the bulletin and a cryptic announcement at the end of Mass. "Anyone interested in joining the R.C.I.A. this year, please e-mail parishoffice@myparish.org or leave a message at the rectory desk." Sometimes parishes might explain what the R.C.I.A. actually is: a wonderful process of grace and discernment that is the normative path of coming to conversion. Sometimes parishes will use words like, "Whoever wants to join the Catholic Church," making the process explicit. But mostly pastors put out bland invitations in the waning summer months, just before September, when more than 75 percent of parishes begin the R.C.I.A. process.

What's behind this blah energy for inviting others? Perhaps we feel conversion is basically an accessory to a person's life, something that might enhance their personal lives but not something that's crucial. Or perhaps we presume that most people will be saved whether they join the Catholic Church or not, and so there is no real need to be energetic about inviting others. Perhaps, too, we feel our Church has relatively little to offer, so if it is offered to a few, then that is good enough. Or maybe we feel most people are already committed to one or another church or faith, so there are few people out there to invite.

I have noticed great differences in the numbers of people who join the Catholic Church. Often the differences arise from location—large parishes in suburbs in the South and West tend to have large numbers interested in joining the Church. One might attribute the difference to that between a diminishing Rustbelt and a flourishing Sunbelt. But this is not always the case. Some parishes in the Northeast and Midwest can garner large numbers of people who want to become Catholic, while parishes nearby settle for a more meager number. I've noticed, too, that numbers in the R.C.I.A can reflect accurately the dynamism of a parish. Those that think of themselves as "holding on" show it in their laid-back approach to everything, including inviting people to the Catholic Church. Those that see themselves as alive and excited, even if they are in rundown areas, seem to attract more people.

If our approach to inviting people is rather passive—God sends us what God sends—then the question of inviting people to conversion is already settled. We take what comes in. But if the question is put another way, namely what participation in the Catholic Church can bring to people's lives, then the issue has a different slant. If the Catholic faith can come as a precious gift, particularly to those living in our modern, secularized American society, how can we *not* invite people to faith? How can we *not* make conversion the basic thrust, not only of our parish, but particularly of our catechumenate?

The Dilemmas of Modern Society

Today, the invitation to conversion happens in an environment crisscrossed with both secular and religious patterns; it happens in a society latent with many contradictory possibilities. I believe that these unresolved tensions form a special opportunity for the Catholic people.

One tension arises from the varied way people look at America as a nation. For most, America stands as an image of the new world begotten at the end of the eighteenth century, when the American colonists threw tea over the side of a ship in Boston, refusing to be taxed as underlings in an empire, and the French Revolution was sweeping away King Louis. For some, America represents something quite different: a system of exploitation in the name of democracy and capitalism, a machine to suck in most of the world's resources and emit most of the world's pollution. Powerful, big, and arrogant, America represents the defeat of a godly way of life for the sake of one that represents greed and lust.

Another tension comes from the way faith and American society have related to each other. Religion, indeed, has been a strange, conflicted bedfellow of America. The scattered approaches of colonial times gave way to a vision of an officially secular state—that is, a state where no one religion would be established and where no religion need exist. At the same time, and some would claim because of its official secularism, America has been home to a succession of religious movements and revivals, making it one of the more explicitly religious societies in the West, at least when it comes to practicing faith. Pilgrim and Puritan adherents, the Great Awakening, Jonathan Edwards, Methodist circuit riders, Catholic immigrants and Catholic revivalism, Prohibitionists and Holy Rollers, charismatics and televangelists: faith has not neglected America.

So a certain ambivalence has evolved between America and its ideals, and between America and faith. Is America genuinely benign, or is it inherently exploitative? Is it instinctively religious, or is it, ultimately, secular? Is modern life the death of belief, or is it a fertile field? Modern Americans carry these questions around in their gut.

These tensions, in particular, occur because of America's relationship to modernity.

Because religion, after the adopting of the Constitution, has always been separated from the state, America enacts the drama of religion and modern life in a paradigmatic way. America represents, perhaps better than most nations, the intersection of modernity with traditional faith, where science, its application and can-do attitude, butts up against transcendence, against the sense that something beyond daily life is necessary to make sense of daily life. Modernity, further, has played itself out in America through processes of urbanization and industrialization, which have augmented the myth of American power. These have challenged a sense of transcendence, a sense that there is something more than everyday life, in the American heart.

- *Urbanization*, with its compressing of people from varying cultures and faith, forced people out of their religious enclaves and engendered an almost forced religious anonymity. People had to downplay their differences to get along. In order to co-exist, in order to get ahead, people in these urban pressure tanks had to suppress what might look particularly provocative to others. In their enclaves, people could identify with a faith; in the "naked square," people knew how to behave. Urbaniza-tion brought everyone to an open, commercialized central city where faith could be supportive, or faith could be forgotten. As Catholics are seeing clearly today, faith changed and came to mean something different when ethnic, European neighbor-hoods sprawled out into the suburbs and disappeared.

- *Industrialization* brought yet another force to bear against a sense of transcendence. It brought, and brings, a sense of pow-er, accomplishment, almost invincibility, as factories produced unlimited goods (and unlimited pollution), railroads snaked across plains and mountains, and assembly lines mechanized both production and the worker. Soon making goods, and making money, would be the purpose of it all. Religion would no longer be the center for people; it would be an add-on to what really engaged Americans—getting rich and buying things. Unions modified some of the more exploitative edges of industry; however, they could not thwart its basic impulses. Religious believers, individually and collectively, have had little impact on the American workplace.

- Finally, *power* plays into the American myth and it too shapes its approach to secularism. America stands for power and the application of this power for what America deems (its) good. The twentieth century saw America grow into the most powerful nation in the world, limited in scope for a while by the Soviet Union, but still capable of blowing the planet apart many times over. That Americans fancy that they use their power only for good hardly tempers the underlying sense that power gives us the notion that we can protect ourselves, deter-mine our parameters, and control our own destinies (and even the destinies of others, if we have to). If prayer to the divine also helps this along, fine. But, basically, God or no God, we will take care of ourselves. In this way, power joined urbanization and industrialization to butt up against transcendence.

As America emerged from its motley collection of colonies ready to form a republic, with motley collections of annexed territories to provide fuel for its expansion, the stage for the great American religious drama was set: immigrants with enormous religious aspirations came to a continent that seemed virtually empty to them. America, the empty stage, was ready to be filled with action, words, music, and story, all to the glory of God. But the very filling up of this stage, the very process of expansion, brought America to the reality of its own exploitation of others and the land and to the very limits of human dreaming. Americans have always sought paradise, whether secular or religious; but America has never attained it.

Amid these conflicting embodiments of the American dream, between its exalted and democratic images and its exploitative and exceptional images, modern people try to make sense of their lives. They are given a public myth revolving around money, around worth being tied to money, around economic theories that correlate hard work with almost manic spending—to keep the economy running. They are given myths, now widely espoused by "the new atheists," pushing a certain view of scientific theories that empty life of much more than accidental meaning. And Americans are also regularly subjected to a religious hucksterism that whips people between shame and innocence. In this way, America begets the main crises that haunt it today: a lack of community and a lack of meaning. Chapter 6 will explore how these are opportunities for Catholic parishes today.

Catholics are called to this modern world, to its dreams and its failures, to its larger myths and its particular stories carved in the actual lives of people. Catholics today have an opportunity to engage this American world with their story of a tradition of faith—not to denounce modernity triumphalistically, not to augment their already large (but decreasing!) numbers, but to give modern people another way to grasp the meaning of their lives. Modern life, with its improvements in health, education, and sanitation, may hide the hungers of the heart very well, but it cannot make those hungers go away.

What can Catholics offer modern society? We offer modern people a solid way to identify with Jesus on a firm road of discipleship.

What Catholics Offer

If modern life catches people with deeply conflicting images of themselves, how can these be resolved? What can modify the tug-of-war between feeling unlimited and the gross limitations that moderns actually face, between wanting everyone to be equal but wanting us to be special nonetheless? What can address the need for power in order to feel secure, and the exploitation of others while everyone feels less secure? What can begin to touch the sense of meaninglessness at the heart of the modern myth that everything is utterly random and the product of blind, material forces?

Catholics can provide a broad space where the tug-of-war conflicts of America can be understood, where the exploiters and exploited can begin to redress the past in reconciliation, where common values can be articulated in ways that allow us our dreams—but also allow us to face reality. Catholics can provide a perspective that allows us to look at ourselves in a way that keeps the bold American vision, but makes it incarnate in the lives of everyday, ordinary people.

For a Catholic believer, this means helping Americans see their destiny in the actuality of the Kingdom of God, in the suffering of the Messiah and the reception of the Messiah's Spirit, in a vision of heaven worked out individually, in human love and compassion. For a believer, this means helping Americans not be deluded by the unbounded horizons that haunt them, but rather helping Americans see that when expansion leads to exploitation, the vision is already lost. For a believer, this means helping our society see that, whatever the drift of the elections, no political party is a messiah, no policy brings salvation, and no promise delivers everything.

Perhaps this is what Christ can best bring most to America: helping it be satisfied with "enough" and keeping it from clamoring for "more" despite the riches it has. Christ can teach us, in the wisdom of the Catholic tradition, that in some ways all are winners and all are losers, but that this only tells us to care more powerfully and directly for each other. Christ can teach us that the Spirit he sends commissions us not to excess but to service, not only to dreams but to actual hope, not merely to success for the few but salvation for the many.

Catholic Assets

Maybe looking at some of the undeniable values in Catholicism can bring new impetus to our desire to share our faith with modern people, particularly those who do not have a faith or involvement in a church. After all, Catholicism embraces that ecumenism that looks for Christians to grow together and eventually become the one Church that professes its one Lord. And Catholicism has committed itself to engage with people of different faiths in dialogue to work together, foster human well-being, and diminish religious antagonism. But, granting this, Catholics need not hide the riches on their table, nor feel ashamed of their abundant gifts.

Consider the following list of assets that Catholics have to offer:

- An unbroken two-thousand year witness to the Gospel
- The Eucharist as unity with God through Jesus, our fundamental worship
- A consistent call to holiness and heroic sacrifice
- A world-wide community of faith and values
- A moral tradition unswayed by fads
- Dioceses and parishes serving people, especially the poor, all over the world
- A constant upholding of the Word of God
- A worldwide network of charity for all people
- An unparalleled commitment to education at all levels
- Profound respect for human reason and natural truth
- Upholding of human rights and dignity
- Deep commitment to human freedom and responsibility
- A communion of all classes, races, and languages
- Active involvement in ecumenical and interfaith dialogue
- The ability to reform and renew itself through God's grace

What other institution, organization, or church can claim a list like this? Often we Catholics have the hardest time seeing the tremendous and unique assembly of values that we have to offer the world today.

Of course, we can look at this list and still think of many problems with Catholicism. We know the complaints frequently made against the Catholic Church, often by Catholics themselves—too unwieldy an institution, unable to change, reactionary, too reliant on authority and power, impersonal and unreasonable. We Catholics have had our scandals, sometimes made to look worse than those of others, but still they are ours. Because of our vast history, we Catholics can always be made to look bad. Nevertheless, these problems do not annul the enormous resources that the Church has, particularly for people today.

If the American nation can ever decide how to guarantee its security or how to gauge its power, perhaps a larger, more "catholic" perspective might help it. If modern society ever decides to deal with issues of exploitation, dehumanization, uncritical faith, human meaning, transcendence, and superficiality, then the Catholic Church has much to offer it. America strives for a kingdom it cannot attain. Our Catholic proclamation of a Kingdom of universal love, so powerfully depicted in the diversity of the Catholic people, may be the message America needs.

America and Catholicism

In some ways, although it may seem counter-intuitive, America and Catholicism may actually be well suited for each other.

Catholicism suits America, and vice versa, because Catholicism complements the American quality of diversity and community, offering a means for a wide variety (of people and experiences) to exist in a broad, cohesive structure. If America has any weak spots, they lie particularly in its inability to affirm equally all its members, and in its illusion of being unlimited; these can deform the very potential of democracy. These weak spots might be darkly amplified as America sees itself as the only superpower, and feels entitled to dictate to the rest of the world. America's weak spots can lead to isolation—either from other nations, or among its citizens.

Catholicism, which spans a spectrum of political styles, powerfully offers a way for individuality and community to exist together. It also offers this in a manner that respects individual freedom and also the autonomy of the state. (This, thanks to Vatican II, is clearer to us than it was in the nineteenth and first half of the twentieth century.) Catholicism has been able to resist the tendency of Christian faith to splinter into a dozen competing and contrasting communities. It also is not identified with any particular state (as, say, Judaism would identify with Israel, or various Orthodox churches with their ethnic nations, or Islam with Saudi Arabia). People have described the Catholic Church as the perfect ecumenical model—diversity and unity. It not only can hold Latin American and African Catholics in unity with Irish Catholics, for example; it can hold folks who tend toward the Mel Gibson part of the spectrum together with those who veer toward Michael Moore's.

Catholicism brings values of morality on both the individual and international levels, emphasizing the personal, as well as the communal, good. Catholicism also brings values that arise from its sacramentality—the goodness of material being—its openness to science, its social commitments to the poor, its tradition of education, and the optimism that arises from seeking the Kingdom of God. While these qualities surely exist in part in some other Christian communities, none holds them together so well as does Catholicism. Catholicism has powerful and unique perspectives to bring to America while, at the same time, being able to resist America's demons of individuality, hedonism (living for the moment and the dollar), and isolation (we can go it alone).

Alternatively, one can credibly argue that America is suited for Catholicism because its form of democracy and social openness are precisely the ingredients to help prevent Catholicism from drifting into its least agreeable excesses—dogmatism, the illusion that authority can settle every conflict, or that uniformity is unity. America can teach the Catholic Church that no matter how much one wants to look at things across centuries, sometimes things need immediate attention. The great lesson that America has taught the world (separation of church and state) is still a novel, but necessary, pill for the Catholic Church to finish digesting. Still, almost seventy million American Catholics show that the pill can be swallowed.

Conversion in Context

When many Americans hear talk of conversion, their suspicions are aroused. Isn't it manipulative, semi-coercive, a playing on weakness? Often modern people, even Catholics, harbor these suspicions about conversion. Yet conversion plays out differently because of Catholic commitment to human freedom and personal integrity. Conversion, in Catholic hands, looks quite different than it does in some evangelical Protestant hands. The Catholic approach entails assumptions well suited to modern life.

Catholics, because of our commitment to the way God works with human freedom, see conversion happening in a human context in which the Spirit works in the hearts of both those who search for, and those who offer, faith. Conversion for Catholics has the following qualities:

(1) Conversion is ongoing, and no one has a monopoly on perfection. In other words, because none of us has crossed the finish line in our present human experience, all conversion is partial, a step toward the fullness that will come only when creation is complete.

(2) Conversion is based in human encounter and has nothing to do with pressuring people. This point is crucial. People share with others in openness; conversion comes about from that starting point. Openness demands, of course, that the believer is touched by the other, even as the believer shares with the other. Conversion cannot happen without a profound respect for the freedom of the other person. If conversion operates in manipulative terms, then the conversion by definition cannot be authentic. To the extent that people experience conversion as a profound exercise of freedom, to that extent conversion can be authentic and bring real change in life.

(3) Conversion takes place in the presumed context of ecumenism and interreligious dialogue. This point is a corollary of point (2). In an encounter with the other, out of profound respect for the other people, one cannot dismiss or dismantle the faith that they have. Catholics believe that God can and does use the faith of another person to bring that person, in some implicit way, into relationship with the Kingdom of God. Even though implicit and incomplete, the Holy Spirit works in the hearts of all who open themselves to God. If people with active faith are nevertheless drawn to another faith experience as a Catholic, this should come as something that builds upon their previous experience. Evangelization never deliberately "targets" a particular religious group.

(4) Conversion builds upon what the Spirit is already accomplishing in a person's life. In other words, if seekers become believers, that is because religious experience is already building upon what God has been doing in their hearts. Although conversion may lead someone to renounce or reject some dimension of a past life, it fundamentally brings to completion the searching that has already been going on. Converts feel that they were always looking for what they have finally found; in this way, conversion affirms a life search. To engage with a seeker means profoundly respecting the Spirit's presence in the other.

(5) Conversion happens within and through peer networks. Conversion hardly ever happens like a thunderbolt from the sky. (Even Paul, when struck with light from heaven, had already been in contact with Christian communities.) Our connections with others, particularly our peer groups, become vehicles through which God works in people's lives. While anonymous encounters may occasionally be moments of grace, most adult conversions happen when people intersect with friends, neighbors, or co-workers. The witness of another's life helps someone see the options and hear an invitation.

(6) Conversion, for Catholics, always has an ecclesial dimension. It arises from our experience of Church, of our being a redeemed people; it expresses itself by relating people to the Church, to the community of the saved, and to its sacraments. Individual people are always in dialogue with other individuals, but faith is never just an individual event. The Church serves as the field for conversion, for our identity in Christ.

So conversion, for us Catholics, is not a sledge hammer. We say that our object is to address the seeker, whether it is someone without a church or someone no longer active in a church. This constitutes our basic approach toward others. To be more precise, we Catholics could never defensibly target a whole group for conversion, such as Jews or Buddhists, or Baptists, because we believe that God leads people in and through various faith experiences. These are people with whom we dialogue. Committed believers in other traditions are not seekers. Catholics pursue conversion in a very "American" way that speaks from the freedom of the heart and its openness to God.

Conversion Today

The call to conversion is both social and personal. The Gospel speaks both to individual hearts and to society itself. Faith has a unique gift to bring to every human heart, and to the broader perspectives through which individuals live.

Modern seekers—a growing phenomenon—will emerge with even greater frequency in the decades ahead. The toll that a soulless, secular vision exacts will only grow more in future generations. People will have a more difficult time finding the most important things they need to live their lives—love, purpose, compassion, selfless sacrifice, optimism, generosity, beauty and all advancement of human progress. These cannot be sustained without a vision of transcendence, how human meaning amounts to more than our simple material existence.

Modern people, too, deal with sin, much as that is hidden and denied by people today. While we can explain away sin, making it all a matter of limitations and mental lapses, we all know how those deeply embedded vices come alive in us every day—greed, lust, anger, pride, hate—all manifestations of selfishness. American fascination with evil shows itself in countless gangster movies and in HBO series like *The Sopranos* or *The Wire*. Nothing can get us beyond the hurdles of our sin except a profound experience of forgiveness, and a constant call to holiness, to growth in virtue, and growth in a sense of union with God.

Because of an absence of compelling religious vision, many people today walk around in semi-stupors, overworked, unconnected, living from day to day, growing distant even from the ones they love, pulled into self-centeredness by society, unable to feel economically secure. They do not have a solid grounding in their lives. The price society pays in terms of dysfunction and destructive behavior because of this deficit of faith cannot be calculated. But it is real, and it may be the greatest factor holding humans back from living in true joy and peace.

Why we keep the Good News to ourselves should puzzle us Catholics. But the reasons not to keep the Gospel to ourselves, the reasons for mission today, challenge our missionary lethargy. If we can let our mission energy rise again, we Catholics can have future years far more positive than those already forecast for us by pundits and experts. Even more, if we can more effectively bestow our sweeping religious and human vision to modern society, the world might well have better decades ahead.

Questions

1. What do you think are unique
   opportunities, and obstacles,
   in American society today that
   affect the call to conversion?
   How do you think modern
   people look on conversion?
   Have you ever felt impelled
   to invite people to think about
   the Catholic Church as an
   option for their expression
   of faith?

2. In what ways do you think
   Catholicism and America
   relate, or can relate, to each
   other? Are there dimensions
   of Catholicism that you feel
   are particularly appropriate
   for Americans? Are there
   aspects of Catholicism that
   might especially be of help
   to modern Americans?

3. What list of assets would
   you make to show how
   Catholicism might appeal
   to people today? What are
   the distinctive marks of
   its credibility for you?
   For people today?

Chapter 3

The Reason for Mission: Our Need to Reach Out

Ever since Pope John Paul II's encyclical *Mission of the Redeemer* was published in 1990, decades ago, Catholics have been, in effect, publicly stating that their idea of mission is in trouble. After all, the fuller title of that encyclical was *On the Permanent Validity of the Church's Mission- ary Mandate,* and John Paul wrote this document to reinforce, or perhaps resuscitate, what had become a rather wobbly mission thrust. Indeed, one often gets the impression that, even where mission is consciously articu- lated, it receives a more "social benefit" justification. Teaching, running hospitals, upgrading the lives of poor people in destitute countries in the name of Jesus—all essential and important tasks in themselves—often seem to rank above explicitly inviting people to the Catholic faith.

A lot has happened since millions of Catholic school children put nickels into cardboard boxes in order to "save pagan babies," the name for the 1950s practice of sending money to foreign missions. Part of what has happened involves a rather massive distancing of many Catholics from any explicit sense of mission, understood as calling unbelievers to Catholicism. Is there a reason for mission? Is there a need for faith? For Christian faith? For Catholic faith? Is there a need for Catholic faith in modern America? One has come to expect long pauses from Catholics in response to questions like these.

Perhaps by directly facing some of the elements that arise in the discussion of this issue of mission, we can begin not only to retrieve dimensions of mission but also invigorate them. For it clearly stands to reason that a church that feels no impulse to invite others into its fold probably has lost some sense of its own meaning, necessity and vitality.

The same elements at work in the universal Church's attitude toward mission are at work, perhaps with even greater force, in our attitude to- ward mission in America, given the way pluralism, commercialism, and secularity have come to dominate the American scene.

Exclusivism

Part of the recoil from an explicit mission stance (meaning an ecclesial stance of feeling an urgency to draw non-believers to one's communion) undoubtedly derives from an embarrassment about a thoroughgoing exclusivism that ran through Christian circles, at least in the Western Church, from the time of St. Augustine through the mid-twentieth-century. This exclusivism arose from a doctrinal position that asserted that, because of the sin of Adam (named "original sin" in Western Christianity), human beings now deserved eternal damnation. Only a few, the exclusive, would be saved from this massive damnation.

This exclusivism drove parents to baptize their children because they were convinced that, without baptism, those children would be destined for hell or, at best, limbo. In a lesser way, exclusivism also drove Christians to feel an injunction to spread the faith to non-believers. I say "in a lesser way" because the damnation of one's own loved ones presses harder on human motivation than the potential damnation of other, stranger and more distant, people.

In this world view, not only were most people going to hell; even more strikingly as things played out, only a few people were going to be saved, even among believers. Sure, God offered grace to "the chosen"—a grace that was represented by membership in the Christian community, the Church both Catholic and Orthodox. Grace, in this way, operated as a specialized selection of a few people because of God's generous, if somewhat arbitrary, choice.

Even among Catholic believers, however, the escape from hell did not seem totally secure because of the ready capacity to seriously sin and thus lose grace. Indeed, as Christianity went through its various expressions of spirituality (monasticism, for example, and, later, Jansenism) and its incorporation of tribal peoples and cultures, the chance for Christians themselves to be saved seemed to diminish. Notions of mortal sin multiplied enough to rival the famous 613 laws of the Pharisees. In medieval, Renaissance, and counter-Reformation periods, it seemed virtually impossible to avoid mortal sin. The pressure from this kind of exclusivism, applied even to believers themselves, was enough to drive Luther to a solution outside the Roman Catholic Church.

Modifications

In the course of the Church's actual pastoral life, however, some of the elements of exclusivism were softened. While Baptism was absolutely necessary for salvation, it also seemed possible that the effects of Baptism might come in other than literal ways. Christians long recognized "baptism by blood," which taught that, should some die for the faith even though unbaptized, they still were saved and would even be considered martyrs. In later history, this form of virtual baptism was extended to intentions: should people live in such a way that they would want to be baptized if they knew of its need, then those people might well be saved. The doctrine of limbo, which is in a kind of limbo itself these days, mitigated the severity of the Christian view that all children who died without Baptism would be damned. This doctrine taught that they were not damned but simply deprived of supernatural happiness because they did not receive supernatural grace.

In the twentieth century, Catholic thinking explored the baptism of desire more fully. The thought that millions of Africans, for example, would forever burn in hell because they did not have the chance to know Christ seemed more unjust to believers in the twentieth century than it had to earlier generations of Christians. Theologians speculated on the salvation of the "Gentiles" more generously than before.

Just prior to the transformative views of the Second Vatican Council, certain theologians began to express things for the unbaptized far more positively. The scriptural passage from 1 Timothy 2:4, which proclaimed, "God wills all people to be saved," seemed more persuasive than a passage like John 3:5, which said that unless someone is born of water and the Holy Spirit, they had no life in them. The great twentieth-century theologian Karl Rahner, SJ, extrapolated on the implications of 1 Timothy by arguing that the will of God to save people had to be an effective will. He linked this assertion with a theory of human nature that situated consciousness itself in a transcendent horizon constituted by God's desire to communicate himself through the Son. Therefore the "obediential potential" for God inside humanity reflected a "supernatural existential" of grace, which bore upon all human beings by virtue of the transcendence shown in their own intellectual and personal searching.

Rahner's position was eventually articulated as "anonymous Christianity": the idea that in some way grace affects the lives of all people, relating them to God through Jesus, even though they might not be aware of it. While certain leaders from other faiths thought that "anonymous Christianity" might be a bit patronizing to believers who were not Christian, the basic thrust of Rahner's position came to dominate both theoretical and popular Catholic thought. Indeed, some of the directions of Rahner's thinking were inscribed in the teachings of the Second Vatican Council itself, which elaborated positions that included (1) people sincerely seeking for God might receive divine grace without being Christian; (2) elements of Catholic life that existed in other Christian communions are authentic vehicles of grace and potential for salvation; and (3) people who were not Christian but who were authentically responding to God through the framework of their religious tradition could be saved as well.

Inclusivism

With a position like this, the impetus behind the frenetic efforts of mission, which had the purpose of saving people from eternal damnation, simply evaporated. What eternal damnation? Was not God ultimately benign and generous, forgiving and loving? Would it be just in any way for God to damn people who had done nothing wrong? Or whose knowledge was not culpable? John Paul II, in his encyclical on mission, expressed two truths that had to be simultaneously maintained: "It is necessary to keep these two truths together, namely, the real possibility of salvation in Christ for all mankind and the necessity of the Church for salvation. Both these truths help us to understand the *one mystery of salvation*, so that we can come to know God's mercy and our own responsibility" (*Mission of the Redeemer*, 9). If, indeed, there is only one Name in whom people can be saved (Acts 4:12), there may be many, and subtle, ways in which that salvation happens.

This change led Christians, and Catholics in particular, to move, virtually within half a century, from a mostly exclusivist tradition, which envisioned the massive damnation of most human beings, to a virtually inclusivist position, which sees salvation as a likely outcome for most human beings who live sincere lives. Indeed, whereas the first Eucharistic Prayer could utter the unworthiness of even believers to be saved ("that we may be delivered from final damnation and counted among the flock of those you have chosen"), the fourth Eucharistic Prayer mentions "all those who seek you with a sincere heart" as one of the groups for whom the Eucharist is being offered. Such an inclusivist perspective not only held out the possibility of salvation for all; it involved, as well, a *presumption* of salvation for almost all people.

Here is the question, then: does an inclusivist perspective actually work, either theologically or pastorally, when one looks at how human beings actually live? I think if we can probe the foundation of a virtually inclusivist viewpoint and discover its weaknesses, we might provide some viable space for looking at mission once again. This, in turn, can lead to some very clear reasons for mission—for inviting people not only to Christianity but also to Catholicism.

Our Human Situation

All thinking about mission has to account for the fundamental thrust of New Testament teaching. This means concentrating not merely on 1 Timothy 2:4 or John 3:5, but on the whole framework that defined the perspective of the first followers of Jesus. One finds nowhere in the New Testament a naïve and unquestioned optimism toward salvation. While modern Christians (except for more fundamentalist strains) generally have not dwelt on the apocalyptic background of first-century believers, the New Testament pulls no punches in sketching a world that not only is coming to an end, but one in which, even more, people will be judged for either eternal life or death. Christian visions of the Apocalypse merged these two elements: God's saving judgment in favor of the righteous, the chosen, would allow Christians to not only escape the tribulation, but also to enter into a new realm called the Kingdom of God. The ending of the Lord's Prayer affirms how prevalent was the sense that humankind would undergo the basic testing that represented the culmination of the force of the Evil one. "Lead us not into temptation, but deliver us from [the] Evil [one]."

In this kind of framework, God's wrath against evil and sin defines the landscape. It is a wrath so dominant that the New Testament constantly preaches against Christian lack of perseverance, that is, falling away from faithfulness to Christ. This theme runs through the parables of Jesus (think of the Sower and the Seed, as well as the Five Foolish Bridesmaids). Even more, a generation before the Synoptic Gospels were written, Paul uses whole sections of the ancient Israelites' experience in the desert to warn the Corinthians about those who did not remain faithful (see 1 Corinthians 10). These Old Testament images are warnings for the Corinthians themselves, lest they not persevere. Salvation certainly is nuanced in the Scriptures and even, in Matthew 25, is something that can happen without a person's awareness. It was by no means a presumption in the early Christian community.

So Christians cannot ignore the reality of sin, a reality that can well distort in the human heart any openness to God, After all, if it is difficult for Christians to be faithful and to persevere in faith, to live with integrity and respond to God's will, how easy can it be for those who do not have the benefits of Christian faith? That is to say, for those who do not have unity with God experienced in the Spirit, the grace of the Scriptures and the sacraments, the witness of moral life and teaching, a community of fellow believers, and the magisterial support of the Church? If the New Testament talks about figures who lived at risk of failure, even though exposed to the Gospel, what does that say for the rest of us?

To be sure, modern people do not expect the imminent end of existence. We do not think of God as "blowing his top," or vindictively lashing out at human beings. We tend not to be apocalyptic. Likewise, modern people are not inclined to be dualists, with such a vivid picture of Satan (almost as an anti-God) that we live in constant dread of demonic wiles.

Nevertheless, we live in the end times; we live with the prospect of judgment. Even granting a modern perspective, which strives to operate without magical or mythic categories, today's Christians have no trouble affirming the following: (1) the intractable forces of evil that form the context of both daily human life and global interaction; (2) divine judgment as both a present and future prospect; (3) God's wrath—seen as the inherent aversion to evil, the negative dynamic of sin; this instinctual aversion is a byproduct of the divine goodness underlying all creation, and built into our human instincts; and (4) the certainty of death, with its consequent dire question of human meaning.

Human existence cannot finesse the ultimate framework of meaning that structures all experience: the utter gift of divine love, freely given, and the implications of failing to receive that love, for every heart and for the world itself.

In view of the eschatological background of the New Testament, reflected in its own way in contemporary theology, *while we cannot presume the damnation of people, neither can we presume their salvation*. To do so would be to deny both the thrust of revelation and the very human reality with which Christianity tries to deal. As a result, the only tenable position for believers is this: **we must proclaim the urgency of the Gospel and call for people to respond to it insofar as they can hear it.** We must call people without faith to discipleship. We cannot leave people without an orientation to the transcendent, nor can we leave people stuck in sin. The Gospel impinges not only on the issue of salvation; it also affects the cognate of salvation, namely the meaning of human existence and human actions.

What we have to resist at all costs is the default, modern secularist, view that human life is an accident of mindless mechanical interactions among atoms and natural forces. With this secular view, we suspend the whole question of human meaning, other than making our human condition more bearable rather than less. Yet the very transcendent dimensions of humankind, revealed in our assumption of meaning, justice, beauty, and love—without which ordinary human life makes no sense—speak powerfully against reducing human existence to blind and inevitable forces. One simply cannot account for ordinary, basic, and deep human behaviors without some reference to an absolute transcendent.

Reasons for Mission

If this perspective (one that is only potentially inclusivist and acknowledges the reality of evil) can be justified, then reasons for mission begin to emerge. There are six of them, each relating to another dimension of revelation or human reality. We have to understand these six reasons in the presumed context of ecumenical and interreligious perspectives, of course, because these perspectives frame all contemporary religious conversation.

Reason #1—The Concrete Offer of Salvation

The Christian Gospel, uniquely, brings humankind solutions to the two dominant problems that beset human experience: the endless entanglement of sin, with all the destruction it brings; and the immovable wall of death. No human life is untouched by the twin threats of sin and death. The basic teaching of the Christian faith addresses these threats by saying that our identification with Jesus Christ brings us into his victory over death, and into the life of his Spirit, which conquers sin.

Although people experience the detrimental consequences of sin every day, they hardly allude to its enormous and gripping power. We join in public outcries against corruption or murder, but we rarely trace these evils to the poverty of our own spiritual lives. Modern people find it easier than ever to deny the impulses toward evil that shape so much of life. Furthermore, we are helpless to even describe the scope of evil as it runs through cultures and generations, bequeathing war, poverty, and the dismissal of human dignity itself. While we sanitize death as much as we can, we are numbed by it and by its relationship to sin.

The Christian Gospel calls people into discipleship, that is, into a new experience framed by salvation. While Catholics do not believe salvation happens completely with conversion, we hold, in every aspect of our Catholic life, that salvation has begun. When we invite people to Christian and Catholic faith, we offer them a Gospel that responds in a unique way to the intractable pull of sin, and one that presents a powerful alternative to the doom of death. In doing so, people begin lives of holiness, of commitment to serving others, and of sharing in God's life in the community of the Church.

When we preach the Gospel, and that Good News is heard, human life is changed. When that Gospel continues to grow in the experience of a person, holiness begins to flourish. When holiness flourishes, then humankind itself is transformed.

The first reason for mission is the dramatic offer of salvation and new life that Christ brought to us, as a possibility for human transformation now and for life into eternity.

Reason #2—Uncovering the Deepest Meanings of Existence

If it is true that people can resolve basic issues in their own lives in some implicit way, that people can live for profound values without explicit religion, this still does not obviate the need to proclaim the Gospel. Rather, this makes it all the more imperative to proclaim the Christian Gospel and invite people to conversion because *Christian doctrines explain the deepest reality of human and divine life.* People may indeed construct some kind of viable account of their human life, even approaching in secular terms the categories that verge on profound Christian themes (forgiveness, altruism, optimism, etc.). But the ultimate reality of our existence can be known only in terms of Christian revelation. To proclaim these doctrines helps all people understand the mystery of their own existence.

Which central Christian doctrines define the ultimate ground of human existence? One would be the *doctrine of the Trinity,* which states that the nature of God is abundant self-gift in generous love. God cannot be understood only as lawgiver, or creator, or cause. For Christians, while indeed worshipping the God of Abraham, God is not a generic term; Christian revelation has made our understanding of God quite specific. The one God is Trinity; the divine is constituted by the dynamic divine relationships. God's self-being, understood as unending generous gift of self to other, lies behind all existence and actually imprints all creation with an inherent drive that moves us beyond self-interest. The nature of being is to live for another, as Father, Son, and Spirit live for other, thereby composing divine life.

The second doctrine that gives meaning to human reality is the doctrine of the *redemption of humankind by Jesus Christ.* This doctrine teaches us that at the heart of human life lies the drama of death and resurrection, the transcendence of our limits because of absolute trust and total love. Jesus lived this drama "for us and for our salvation," as we say in our Creed, opening up for humankind the prospect of transcendence beyond death in his resurrection. That is to say, Jesus not only dies because of our sin; he is raised for our sin and for our salvation, for only in resurrection does the full drama of human existence unfold. One cannot overstate the implications of this doctrine in terms of suffering, hope, and life beyond death. This doctrine teaches us the ultimate pattern of human life and meaning, quite in distinction to various modern approaches to the meaning of life.

The third crucial doctrine, implied in the second, is that of the *incarnation* whereby we teach that the Second Person of the Trinity was united through the person of the Son with the human reality of Jesus. Besides showing the dynamic, self-less unfolding of the divine which the Trinity shows us, this doctrine also states that, in some mysterious way, human nature itself can be an apt expression of the reality of God. This insight buttresses claims that human nature cannot be reduced to mere material reality, an essential message for modernity.

To remain silent about these doctrines, which affect the very meaning of existence, would deprive humans of those teachings that allow them to have the best account of their lives, their morality, their hopes, and the ground of their being. Of course, other doctrines—of the sacraments, the

Church, moral life and human dignity—also describe basic truths about human experience, but they rest on our teaching about God and Jesus.

Reason #3 —Liberation

Christianity expresses a pattern of redemption that can be applied to the powerful ways in which human beings find themselves trapped. Because it is about transcendence even through death, the Christian Gospel can liberate people from those things that constrict human life in its most fundamental dimensions. The pattern of death and resurrection is translated, in human activity, into the pattern of slavery and freedom.

People, after all, get stuck in systems of addiction, compulsion, anger, sin, depression, and despair that act like bars imprisoning their lives. Such entanglements are not rare events. People often find themselves in predicaments that call for them, in the imagery of William James, to be "twice born," as we saw in chapter 1. They have reached a dead end; they need to experience rebirth.

Conversion, to be sure, can come in many forms. Not everyone experiences Christian life as a breakthrough from near-total confinement in life; some people are, as William James put it, "once born," without a sense of brokenness or despair. But others need to be "twice born"; the Christian Gospel, with its message of death and resurrection, responds to these needs in compelling ways. The experience of being radically forgiven, and of being able to start over again in present human experience, to be freed from addictions and crippling vices, comes as an unmatched grace for people. This happens through an experience of identifying with Jesus Christ in the Holy Spirit. Even those who sense themselves as "once born" still have some patterns of being trapped in their lives.

Articulating a call to conversion, then, allows people in desperate need to find a breakthrough that otherwise might not be available to them. Insofar as conversion is the development of a fixed commitment, through the grace of God, to live for the Kingdom of God, when people come to conversion in such a dramatic and life-changing way, the power of the Christian gospel becomes transparent. What people experience in recovery programs like Alcoholics Anonymous and Narcotics Anonymous derives, in essence, from the Gospel of Jesus. Here, then, is a third reason to proclaim the Gospel.

Reason #4—Expressing the Depth of Christian Vocation

Another reason to invite people to faith involves helping them achieve a vision of themselves as living vicariously, as representatives, for others. In other words, Christians work out in their individual lives the drama of all human existence; in doing this, they help all humanity get some sense of God's love and, in some way, begin to experience this love. Individuals' conversions, and communities of the converted, prefigure a more universal transformation. Believers, through their faith, have the privilege of helping carry all of humankind toward the Kingdom.

Christian and Catholic life is, after all, a vocation, a state of being chosen. Catholics receive a calling analogous to the call received by people in the Scriptures. When we are baptized, we receive our "name" before God, our vocation as disciples. To be called, however, is to be called to serve others, to live on behalf of others, to carry in one's own life the burdens and destiny of others. Everyone whom God chooses in the Scriptures is not chosen for him- or herself. Rather, they are chosen for the sake of others: so too with the call to be baptized and become a disciple of Jesus Christ.

Think of Abraham, the one "in whom all the nations of the world" would find blessing. Think of Isaac, his son, who contends with God and is tested so that he can be the father of his people, Israel. Moses, likewise, is snatched from death so he might be the liberator of his fellow Jews, enslaved in Egypt. The Jewish people are called as emblems of God's liberation of all humankind. God does not call the prophets for their own sake, but to bring hope, consolation, and correction to their fellow believers. We find some prophets, like Jeremiah and Amos, complaining that their lives were simpler before they were called to prophesy; their ministry was a labor undertake on behalf of others.

The ultimately chosen one is Jesus, the Son of God, "my beloved, my chosen," in whom all humankind is chosen. Jesus is the New Adam, the new form of humankind that becomes a possibility for all those who have unity and identity with him. Paul himself sometimes comes close to universal language, talking about Jesus as the new man in whom "all are saved" (see Romans 5:15). Jesus lives vicariously on behalf of all humankind to bring reconciliation with God, forgiveness of sin, and new meaning to human existence.

With Jesus, so all the Church is called to the special grace of living vicariously for the world. If believers can carry others to salvation, to the inner being of God, to the Kingdom—even if others are unaware of this—then these believers, too, are chosen instruments of God on behalf of the world. Christians are sacraments, through whom God is bringing salvation to the world. In them, it happens knowingly and as a vocation, a service; in others, it happens by their implicitly being touched by the call of the Kingdom.

To invite people to this special grace of living vicariously for others is to bring them into a special identification with God. Discipleship, then, is a service on behalf of others, a life of service and love in the image of Jesus, who gives his life for the many, and for the redemption of the world. To be a disciple is to enact that redemption in actual life.

Reason #5—To Invite People to Salvation in the Kingdom

A fifth reason for mission entails the insight that discipleship actually is life in the Kingdom of God, experienced in an inchoate way even in this life. In our lives as disciples, the Kingdom is already being experienced. In the Word of God, in the sacraments, and in the fellowship that Christians experience, believers are bringing about in present categories the realities that will define the fullness of the Kingdom. When we call people to conversion, we are calling them to experience salvation as freedom from sin and union with God.

This resonates with the apocalyptic sense of the New Testament. Faith is a life-or-death decision. There are no fences on which Christians can sit; belief is a decision, a choice for the Kingdom, a choice for God as revealed in Jesus. The decision of belief has an impact in this life and, beyond this life, in eternity.

One Christian temptation has been to think of the Kingdom in purely future terms, or in terms that imply distance. So the Kingdom will come, Christians say, when the Lord comes a second time. Or people enter the Kingdom after they die. Such thoughts, while faithful to some of the language of the New Testament, overlook other dimensions of New Testament teaching, in which the Kingdom is declared to be "among you" or "right at hand."

It is perfectly coherent to think of the Kingdom as the ultimate dimension of all existence, including present existence. When people are open to God, the Kingdom that is all about them is unveiled. That is what the ministry of Jesus consisted in: uncovering the dimensions of the Kingdom before our very eyes—in the healings, the freeing from demons, the declarations of divine forgiveness and mercy, the teachings of the Kingdom in parable and discourse, and in the outline of what it means to be a disciple.

What we will be forever before God begins in how we exist presently before God. We begin eternal life right now; through the structures of discipleship we begin to live forever. Hearing the Scriptures means we think in divine patterns; committing ourselves to Christ's way means we begin defeating evil; receiving the sacraments means we re-enact Christ's encounter with humankind in our own lives; prayer results from our being touched by the Spirit of God in our actual life; sharing love in Christian community betokens a final state of universal community.

So how can we let people live without inviting them to begin eternal life, life with God, in an explicit way, right now? How can we pass up the chance to give others an experience of what God offers to everyone: abundant life? Some Protestant Christians have taught that one could know that one was chosen by the blessings received in this life. It is far more likely that the case goes like this: one can know one has begun life in the Kingdom by living as a disciple of Christ. "I have come that they may have life, and have it abundantly (John 10:10)."

Reason #6—The Scope and Fullness of the Catholic Church

Thus far, we have seen multiple reasons for mission, for inviting people to the Catholic faith. This faith offers eternal life, clarifies human meaning, frees people from what entraps them, provides a chance to live vicariously for others, and gives them a present, initial experience of the Kingdom. Catholics have a particular reason for mission, one that arises from the nature of Catholicism itself.

Catholics have reason to undertake mission in a powerful way because Catholicism contains the *universal scope* and *spiritual fullness* that best express Christian teaching and life. Catholicism best embodies the ideals of the Kingdom, both present and to come.

Discipleship, after all, by its very nature has *universal* dimensions. All people are called to be disciples, and all are called to be involved in the making of disciples. Catholicism, because of its roots and reach, expresses most clearly this universal discipleship. Tracing its roots (along with the Orthodox Churches) to the earliest apostolic traditions, the Catholic

Church transcends both nationalism and regionalism. It embodies, more clearly than all other Christian experience, the vision of Matthew 28:10: "Go and make disciples of all the nations. . . ." Its universality allows for multiple paths: some for "the many," who find holiness in daily life, and some for "the few," who find holiness in structuring their whole existence around gospel ideals and explicit witness.

Beyond its universality, Catholicism has a *fullness* that contains all forms of Christian expression. It can relate to all Christian traditions. Its fullness allows it to find rapport with the high ecclesiology of some Christian expressions, with those that emphasize the Word of God as a force for conversion, with Pentecostal expressions of faith, and with communions that emphasize their congregational nature. In its teaching, practice, and actual living, Catholicism shows itself to contain, in a paradigmatic way, the fundamental elements of Christianity. Its sacramental, Spirit-filled, scriptural, spiritual, organizational, and magisterial expressions all enrich the Catholic ability to reveal the fullness of Christian life.

The Catholic Church, because of its history and tradition, contains the fullness of Christian revelation and the fullness of the means of salvation. It lives this reality by sharing its rich and unique tradition in a universal and complete way.

This does not deny that Catholicism has had its problems. One can point again and again in history to the need for reform and renewal in the Catholic Church. Nevertheless, such a realization also shows that the Catholic Church has exactly that capacity to reform and renew itself. Whether it is through bottom-up spirituality or top-down projects of reform, Catholicism has been able to preserve in itself the elements necessary for full Christian life. If other communions, at any given time, express one or another element more powerfully than Catholicism, this still means that those other communions received their blessings in some way from the living Catholic tradition.

Ecumenical and Interfaith Perspective

Vigorously affirming the universal dimension of mission does not deny that people can be saved without being Catholic. Nor does it deny the special spiritual dimensions and truths that exist in other Christian communions and, indeed, in non-Catholic faiths. Catholics affirm elements of grace not only in other Christian communions but also in non-Christian traditions. Catholics affirm that the Holy Spirit is at work throughout the world in ways that are clear, and also in ways mysterious and unknown.

Further, Catholics talk about ecumenism in mission language (that is, as evangelization) because they see ecumenism as a way for all Christians to live more fully in obedience to the Word of God, with the consequent purification of distortions that will come from that obedience. In ecumenism, we hear the Gospel more deeply. In ecumenism, we share, from our respective traditions, our witness to the Gospel and its effects. Beyond ecumenism, Catholics find in inter-religious dialogue a profound opportunity to witness to the power of faith in Jesus, even as they hear the sincere expressions of other faiths.

Affirming these truths does not, however, annul the call to mission. Rather, it focuses the scope of mission primarily upon those who have no religious tradition and those who have, in effect, given up practicing and living their faith, both growing segments in modern America. In a world where the rising tide for one boat means that all boats are rising as well, the call to deeper conversion and more explicit discipleship through Catholic mission can only strengthen all expressions of faith.

Mission

Mission, in the phrase of John Paul II, is permanently valid. The Kingdom, the goal of all humankind, will bear upon all people with more explicit power the more it is revealed in human life. Mission does not take away from people what they have; rather, mission offers people what they need, whether they know it or not: the deepest patterns of human and divine life, power for transformation, a life of discipleship focused on living for others, an actualization of the Kingdom in its initial expressions in our present life, and a vision of church that is universal and full.

Perhaps not everyone need be a Christian; God's grace is broader and subtler than many Christians have realized. Perhaps some dimension of universal salvation has always been implied in Christian life. Granting all those possibilities, what is actual and certain is this: to call those without faith to Catholic and Christian life is to offer them resources for life's needs and its fulfillment.

Why not do it?

Questions

1. What are your own assumptions about salvation? Do you think of yourself as more "exclusivist," presuming that only good Catholics can be saved? Do you think of yourself as more "inclusivistic," tending toward belief that almost everyone will be saved? How do you clarify your viewpoint?

2. What are the more powerful reasons for mission that you experience in your pastoral life? What are the ones that you find motivate people to spread the Good News of Jesus? How would you express the reasons for mission?

3. How do you relate our Catholic commitment to ecumenism and interfaith dialogue with an absolute commitment to mission?

4. Do you think the energy for mission has lessened? If so, why? What do you feel about this?

Chapter 4

American Culture and Catholic Parishes

Is there an American form of religion? I believe there is.

While the Jewish Reform movement might be the best evidence of Jewish inculturation in America, and while it will be interesting to see how Islam comes to relate to American culture, there undoubtedly is an American form of Christianity, a form that has grown more pronounced and robust in the past fifty years. Some of this American form of Christian religion derives from the twentieth-century Pentecostal movement, with its emphasis on gifts and exceptional signs. Nevertheless, the primary expression of Christian faith in the United States can stand on its own, apart from Pentecostalism. Indeed, modern Pentecostalism, when it began more than a century ago, might have had its success because of how deeply it drank from streams of American religion.

Before we look at some of the more obvious traits of American religion, it bears noting that all expressions of faith based on ritual (i.e., celebrating a form of the Lord's Supper regularly) are being challenged by these elements of American religious style. In other words, Lutherans and Episcopalian-Anglicans, and other groups that have developed clear patterns in their order of worship, mostly around celebration of the Eucharist, face challenges similar to those faced by Catholics. Why? Because formal ritual is not easily adapted to this American style of religion.

It has always struck me as strange that evangelism, so typical of American religion, could claim such broad success when what it has basically done is to move a Christian from one ecclesial group into another ecclesial group. Clearly, though, this is what often happens in those circles of church that claim the name "evangelical." To have their congregations filled with Catholics, Lutherans, Methodists, and other Christians from mainline church groups seems more like a conversion to style rather than a conversion to faith. Evangelicals might rightly point to how they have made rather listless Christians into more active and enthusiastic believers, and have moved some believers who occasionally practice their faith to more consistent worship. But at the same time evangelicals have to ponder how faith has become unmoored from loyal footings that more traditional churches provided. This kind of unmooring might well, in the long run, lessen loyalty to any religious tradition; in fact, we may be seeing that in the upsurge of more explicitly secular stance, particularly among the young. In America, church has become relative, a matter of preference; this has inevitable and somewhat frightening implications.

Elements of American Religion

Let me list and elaborate on five of the more overt elements of American religion. I take these from aspects of the larger megachurches, which seem to have tapped into the American religious stream quite powerfully; but these elements can characterize smaller congregations as well. After developing these five areas, I will begin outlining the invitation they provide for our Catholic parishes in America.

(1) Experience

American faith now consists primarily of personal experience, based on what people feel and what people think they should be feeling. Once the criterion of faith becomes only "the Word," unattached to any particular tradition transmitting that Word, then preachers, congregations, and believers can take from the Word seemingly endless variations based on very elastic criteria. The Word, and its various interpretations, can be infinitely plastic, presenting a wide range of logical, linguistic, and emotional palettes. If nothing apart from the Word guides it or puts it into context, then any reading, and adaptation, of the Word will seem as good as any other. Perhaps this is the inevitable consequence of thinking that the Scriptures are self-interpreting. Nevertheless, because of this American element of faith, so-called external criteria like history, tradition, *magisterium,* or ritual, which we Catholics think are slam-dunks in religious conversation, cannot pack much of a punch in today's world.

Another important dimension of experience is how it has an eminently emotional ring to it. Surely the American religious experience has obvious social factors (the congregation, my friends, my family), but our American version emphasizes almost exclusively the personal, inner drama of pain/ brokenness/need, with a story of unexpected relief from that dreadful complex of feelings. The relief entails a feeling of freedom, exaltation, enthusiasm, and assurance. Notice how gradually, throughout the twentieth century, Christians moved from language of certainty (our Catholic drive to infallibility came from the nineteenth-century version of this impulse) to a concern with assurance. Certainty speaks to the mind; assurance speaks to the emotions. It seems clear that, in American religion, the need for assurance trumps the needs of the mind in priority and importance, at least in terms of initial appeal. One can see how this appeals to the various layers of insecurity and individuality that form a matrix on the American scene, as we saw in chapter 2.

(2) Congregationalism

A second element of American religion is its congregational instinct. This derives, in part, from a democratic thrust in the culture that resists institutions as well as all things that seem to intrude on the individual, thereby making institutions suspect. Because American religion articulates itself so clearly in experiential terms, one theoretically never has a need for any church, even a congregationally-based one. "I'm personally saved," is how the experience goes. So if there is any impulse toward gathering with other believers, one picks a congregation according to one's preference. Churches, in this view, fundamentally serve the purpose of sustaining a particular experience. Just as experience is individual, so also is choice about a church setting.

So in American religion, allegiance may be to the pastor, or to the setting of one's fellow worshippers, but not to a larger concept of church. This explains the success of so-called non-denominational churches, as well as the marketplace attitude toward church. We can make church up as we want, and we can tailor church to our wants and desires. The democratic thrust shows itself in the congregation's electing its leaders, hiring its pastors, and choosing the priorities of the congregation. The idea that a congregation might have to be authorized by a larger church group would seem only an add-on to a large number of Americans. Hence the saying in some places: "When you lose your job, well, you can then start a church."

(3) Worship

Worship is the third element of American religion—here, for the purposes of contrast, sharply distinguished from liturgy. I use the word "worship" as the structured set of events that induce in participants a certain range of feelings. Evangelical congregations are characterized by a "praise ministry," which produces a medley of hymns and songs, all of which strike emotional notes, with crescendos amplified by trumpets, drums, and occasionally violins. To describe this as entertainment, as some priests do, hardly does justice to what people in these churches think is happening. But entertainment, in the basic sense of keeping a service moving and inducing a set of feelings in people, certainly is a part of what is happening. How far this seems from Catholic experience can be gauged by the way priests cringe when a parishioner says, "Father, that was a good Mass today." Isn't it, we want to say, a good Mass every day?

We need to notice how differently liturgy functions from worship. Liturgy certainly has its aesthetic and potentially emotionally parts; any priest who has held the cross as it is being venerated on Good Friday has certainly seen emotion. But the emotional effect of liturgy is quite secondary. Because of its rather neutral and predictable structure, liturgy allows people to bring to it almost any set of emotions, from their differing personal emotional places. Whether anxious, happy, newly engaged or newly grieving, Catholics can bring almost any personal state into the Mass; good moods find a place in Catholic liturgy, as do edgier moods. Liturgy's sober quality can be open to many feelings. Liturgy does not try to induce a feeling; rather, it elaborates a broad pattern of death-and-resurrection that permits all human experience to find resonance in it.

(4) Relationship

Because American religion is experiential, relationship is an essential element. Even though faith is personal, believers, if they choose to congregate with others, want to feel positive contact with others. The presence of other congregants affirms each individual's state. Despite the fact that some congregations on the American model can be very large, congregants are still able to feel a particular bonding with others—a bonding reinforced by the way people welcome and greet each other, as well as by the multiple associations people can form with like-minded believers, particularly in the larger churches. This is the secret to megachurches, some of which claim tens of thousands of members. They encourage association in smaller groupings, whether the purpose is to share Scripture, to talk about parenting, to be involved in a particular sport, to extend recovery from addiction, or some other reason.

The commercial sector of America has caught the sense of hospitality very well. How people are received in an office, how they are greeted when coming to a restaurant or even to a Wal-Mart, how they are responded to when they have a complaint—all of this defines the basic way American society operates in its business practices. Perhaps it is the anonymity of American life, or the very choice-based dynamics of suburban life, which mandates making overt the connections people have with one another. Evangelical churches understand this feature of American public life and have adapted it quite well.

These elements of experience and relationship form the ground of what has become the American version of Christianity—namely, "accepting Jesus as your personal Lord and Savior." The only other factor in American religion that might trump this is the phenomenon of "being born again in the Holy Spirit," which drives the emotional, experiential, and relational dynamics of faith to very explicit dimensions. Even apart from the basic social aspects of relationship, people can feel connected to others because they, too, have experienced Jesus, or the Spirit, "just as I have." The part of Catholic experience that may be analogous to this is Holy Communion: when Catholics are intensely conscious of the Christ they have received, they can also be conscious of the reception of Christ by all who have partaken in the Eucharist. In some way, the more classical expression of the Mystical Body of Christ, developed in the 1950s, caught this better than many modern ecclesial expressions.

(5) Marketing

One last conspicuous element of American religion is marketing. The approaches of American evangelism often come down to this: segments of the society are targeted for recruitment to particular congregations. More than the way congregations routinely send letters to people who move into their neighborhood, marketing means doing demographic studies, finding out the ages and dispositions of people in a particular area, and developing a congregation to appeal to just such a demographic niche. While such marketing is admittedly buttressed by the efforts of individual congregants to reach out to friends and neighbors, the premise of American religion is that people can be induced to join a church by techniques such as mailings, home visits, telephone campaigns, and public media. After the pastor has formed a nucleus of people who are part of the founding congregation, he or she can build a larger congregation on the basis of this initial grouping.

The "4 Laws of Effective Outreach," a CD-Rom collection issued by www.outreach.com, specifies the rules as follows: 1) Attract and invite people; 2) Form people in faith; 3) Involve people in the congregation; and 4) Get people to invite others. The first law gives ample evidence of the explicit marketing dimension of evangelical expressions of faith. No honest observer, surely, would see evangelism only as marketing; rather, marketing would form one of the many tools a Christian might use to bring another person to Christ. "Bringing someone to Christ" means helping people experience personally a sense of salvation from the various burdens that are part of human life, particularly when salvation comes in the form of an experience of relief from an overwhelming threat.

While this list cannot do justice to the complex reality of religion in America, I think it does catch some of its basic foundations. When Americans, by and large, think about faith, they gravitate toward these kinds of traits.

What do these traits, then, have to say to American Catholic parishes?

The Catholic Parish

Since we Catholics now operate in the broad matrix of what I've termed American religion, we do not have the luxury of thinking about our parishes as if this broader religious environment did not affect us directly. Studies consistently show the steady erosion of Catholics, at least from the practice of their faith if not from the Catholic faith altogether. Anecdotal information often confirms just how many "ex-Catholics" are attending some new evangelical or non-denominational church in the neighborhood. Whatever motivates Catholics in this direction, it certainly is not our central dogmas of faith, nor is it our sacramental practices. Catholics do not leave because of the Incarnation or the Eucharist. They leave, rather, because our Catholic parishes seem unable to respond to the implicit directions of faith in modern life. Our parishes seem more like hold-outs from a former time, when faith was based on cultural identity—with all the assumptions about church that go along with that—rather than congregations responsive to how modern people think of religion.

I believe that we Catholics can respond to some of the directions of American religion, without, of course, capitulating to assumptions about faith that cannot be sustained theologically, pastorally, or historically.

Further, I think that unless Catholic parishes begin to respond in some of these directions, we risk becoming an enclave of older people in an ever-smaller church. I further believe that Latinos, whose presence among us has kept our numbers from outright plummeting, will soon expect parishes to adopt a more modern style of church, replete with aspects of American religion as I've sketched it. I want to touch on the elements of American religion with reference to what they might have to say to Catholic parishes today.

(1) Experience

Catholics have to start getting comfortable with their experience of faith by recognizing it, owning it, and expressing it more clearly. While American religion offers a foundation that is primarily experiential, and often articulated in the form of inner crisis and emotional relief, Catholics can point to a far more solid basis: experience grounded on the Word of God and the sacred signs (sacraments), which have structured Christian life from the beginning. In the long run, when inevitable questions about an experience-only faith are raised in earnest, Catholics will have a lot to offer to the discussion of religion in America. We Catholics can put experience into context.

Any reflection on Christian life can easily sustain the notion that personal experience has always been in the context of a community of faith that understands itself as descended from the apostolic tradition. Such communities of tradition are hardly inimical to personal faith; rather the opposite is true. Personal faith is difficult to sustain without communal support. What Catholics can offer is both deep experience and the external criteria that have upheld Christian experience from the beginning. This Catholic perspective offers protection from some of the potential narcissism that can often accompany a primarily personal articulation of faith. How easily, in the American religious idiom, salvation can come across as what God has done "for me," or how God has "blessed me" with abundant riches—as if the Kingdom were directed primarily at making individuals feel better. Catholicism, with its unfolding of Christian faith in terms of community and service, can correct some of these misplaced emphases.

None of this, however, relieves Catholics of the need to deal with personal experience. Doing this is imperative. Catholics need to emphasize the experiential elements in our Catholic life; and we need to expand our repertoire of personal religious experience. We tend to identify almost entirely with the Sunday Eucharist or, for a very small percentage of believers, with eucharistic adoration. We have to help Catholics identify authentic faith experiences in various parts of their lives—with personal prayer, the Word of God, moral life, family life, relationships with others, and the various ways Catholics experience the Holy Spirit. Pastoral leaders, from priests and deacons in their preaching, to directors of faith formation, need to help Catholics develop the perspective and vocabulary to make clearer for them the personal elements of our faith experience.

(2) Liturgy

In place of worship as I outlined it above, Catholics put forth *liturgy* as the tradition-rooted expression of divine presence in the community of faith. Rather than being construed as a church service to bring about certain emotions, liturgy is a rite that enables people to bring a range of experiences and emotions into the Paschal Mystery of Christ's death and resurrection. Rather than possibly manipulating people's emotions, liturgy, in its transparent but sober form, permits a range of emotions, without making emotion, or feeling, the goal. Catholics can point to a whole host of mystics who have insisted that spirituality cannot grow if it remains in its "affective" form—this insight, in itself, would be an enormous contribution to (and correction of) American religion.

That being said, it remains true that the more evangelical dimensions of faith that are latent in our liturgy need to be more consciously exposed and celebrated. Christ does call us together. The Word does call us to conversion. The homily does challenge us to renewed commitment. The offertory does demand that we give our very selves to God. The Eucharist does insist that we become the Body of Christ. The dismissal does commission us for discipleship in the world. Nothing in our theology or liturgical practices excuses our boring people, or calls us to make faith into a set of wooden external gestures.

Nor do we Catholics need to be content only with the Eucharist as a form of worship. From holy hours, to prayer nights, to retreat days, to parish missions, to small-group sharing, Catholics need to be invited to a range of options where feelings can be surfaced and expressed—and brought to God. Can it be that, by defaulting everything to the Sunday Eucharist, we are somehow short-changing the Catholic people?

(3) The Parish

While congregational tendencies have become stronger in today's Catholics, who seem to identify more with the local parish than the local church (the bishop), the missionary roots of our notion of Catholic parish have to be acknowledged and reinvigorated today. Similar to congregations in the American religion model, Catholic parishes also reinforce personal experience. But Catholic parishes explicitly carry the mandate of the bishop as part of their very charter and, as a result, have an outward direction toward mission that should speak to every level of parish organization. We should not see this episcopal mandate only in organizational terms, as if somehow Catholic chanceries were mission bases. Rather, as the bishop's mandate calls for sharing the Good News with everyone in his diocese, and inviting all to the table of the Lord (however idealistic that may be), so parishes have built into their constitution the same universal mandate for mission. Parishes simply do not exist for themselves.

Because Catholic life is, by definition, rooted in the diocesan reality, Catholicism can offer something broader and deeper than a congregation with a leader. Catholics bring a commitment to a whole territory, with an array of ministries and services that address a whole territory, served by an assembly of ministers that include bishops, priests, deacons, religious, and married and single lay faithful. The *cathedra* of the bishop serves as a common focal point of unity and mission. The Catholic task is not merely to cultivate unity in one's congregation, but rather to build a network of unity that is open to all, both believers and potential believers. The more religious leaders make this universal missionary mandate of the diocese clear to everyone, the more our Church can be perceived less as a tradition-bound sluggish institution and more as a sign of the universal desire for communion inherent in the human heart.

This may help those dioceses and parishes that have to deal with phenomena that we call "clustering," or "merging," or "downsizing" parishes. The trauma associated with these moves is notorious; people feel torn from their church building and, therefore, also torn from their faith. We need to emphasize, as an ordinary part of Catholic life, identifying with the bishop's apostolic mandate, and with the way parishes connect with the diocese. Then Catholics would have not only parish as their main identity; they would begin to think more broadly.

(4) Relationship

Unfortunately, it may come as a surprise to Catholics, clergy and lay, to learn that their parishes are essentially relational groupings. Parishes have, in themselves, relational vectors, which play out in numerous ways. Perhaps some parishes think of themselves *primarily* as organizations/institutions—and some of them are certainly large enough to justify such categorization. But even our largest, megachurch-like, parishes primarily operate, knowingly or not, in smaller relational patterns. We need to let these relational patterns stand out more clearly.

How people experience each other profoundly colors their sense of church. The presence, or absence, of welcome and greeting speaks volumes—about parishioners and how they see themselves, and to visitors, about how they are seen by parishioners. But it has to go even beyond this: people in our pews have to feel connected to each other. Some of this is intangible, but no less real. Other aspects are quite tangible. The way we go about registering people in parishes, the contact we have with young families and young adults, the access children and teens have to our parish—all of these add shades to the overall color that our parishes have. Parishes need warmer human colors to attract and sustain involvement today.

Although half of Catholic parishes are the size of megachurches (2000 members or more), very few have exploited some of the practices of megachurches that might make sense for us Catholics. Paradoxically, the immigrant church between 1850-1950 functioned as a version of today's megachurch. With nickels and quarters, Catholics parishes provided an amazing range of services to struggling immigrants. Priests and nuns served as on-site ministers, hosting dances, supervising sports, engaging parents, providing social referrals and, principally, educating people for a promising future in the American experiment.

People need to connect with each other; I will explore this more fully in chapter 5. This needed ingredient, by itself, keeps us from dissolving into isolated bubbles of TV-watchers or iPod listeners. Church has to play a role in this. Today many parishes do provide a range of services. However, a real priority needs to be fostering connections among parishioners in small groups, in self-help processes, and in areas of common concern. Catholics, with our commitments toward a social experience of faith, should be giving leadership in this. Unfortunately, we are not. The style of American religion has much to show us.

It goes without saying that Catholic leaders have to help their people appropriate the personal relationship they have with Christ. Even more, we can put that relationship into its fuller biblical context because relationship with Christ is oriented to the Father, embedded in the experience of the Holy Spirit, and oriented to the Kingdom of God. Can anyone provide a keener living commentary on Matthew 7:21 than we Catholics? "Not everyone who says to me, 'Lord, Lord,' will enter the kingdom of heaven, but only the one who does the will of my father in heaven." As Matthew puts it, it is not primarily a matter of personal experience, but how personal experience is shaped and used to meet the demands of the Kingdom of Heaven.

(5) Marketing

When it comes to marketing, Catholics, as a group, are perhaps most out of the loop. We hardly do it. When we do it, we begrudgingly spend pennies and expect landslides in return. As a result, our image in America gets shaped by others—the stereotypes on television and radio, the innuendo in even the most respectable news media. Meanwhile Catholic media employ the kind of ecclesiolatry that characterizes most of our diocesan newspapers, with images of mitered and surpliced figures dominating everything else.

Even worse, we Catholics have not connected with the hunger that drives the relentless American search for the spiritual and how Catholicism can respond to that hunger in powerful ways. Our invitations to the R.C.I.A are mostly whispers. We hardly announce beyond our bulletins wonderful spiritual offerings happening in our parishes. So people pass by our churches without a clue to what the Church can be offering them. Saddest of all, many of these people passing by our churches were themselves baptized Catholic.

While we may be reluctant to, as it were, sell ourselves, we really have no choice but to powerfully upgrade the profile of our most important message: that we are a community of Gospel, of grace, of mercy, and welcome. We have to project images of ourselves beyond that of rule-driven obsession that often is the first, and last, impression people have of us. We have to show the smile, the embrace, the warmth, the acceptance that lies at the base of true Catholic experience. I was quite heartened recently to hear Archbishop O'Brien of Baltimore on the radio asking people to think about vocations. The final line of his pitch went something like this:

"Our hearts and doors are always open." Now if a message like this could be amplified across America, we Catholics might begin to start looking different to others (and maybe even to ourselves).

The Future

One of the illusions we have as a Church is that if we do one thing or another, then the 1950s will come back, as if this were somehow the real objective of evangelization. We need to look forward, not backwards, because the social reality in which we live, and will live, is nothing like the social reality out of which older Catholics have come. We will be, like it or not, more a product of choice than culture. We will be (and already are) one more choice that people can make in today's market-driven world. We will have to wear our relationships openly, be more direct in our experience, and more expressive in our tradition.

Catholics cannot, and should not, be evangelical Protestants. It is hardly our role to dress in theological and pastoral garments that will never, and should never, fit us. Indeed, some of the dynamics of evangelical Protestantism might begin to wane just as surprisingly as they emerged in American experience. That being said, we will have to start seeing how our tradition and commitments as a Church can be enhanced by what has emerged in the form of what I describe as American religion. We need to do this because eventually this American form may well be part and parcel of the experience of faith in most of the modern world, since it appears to be spreading well beyond America. If anything ever recaptures Europe, perhaps it will be a form of Catholicism healthily stamped by the American experience. It seems that what people find attractive about African, Asian, and Latino expressions of Catholicism are the liveliness and communal character.

My purpose with these words is hardly to extol uncritically American religion; I trust I have pointed out many of its flaws. Nevertheless it is the environment in which we live and serve. Understanding the contours of this environment, and seeing which parts of it we can turn to our own advantage and even to our own betterment, can only further the evangelizing task that the Lord has placed upon us all. Our next chapter explores what a future might look like, given the experience of younger generations of Americans.

Questions

1. What do you consider the particular opportunities and limitations of Catholic parishes today in the United States? How you do you think most Catholics feel about their parishes?

2. If Catholic parishes cannot become evangelical congregations, how do you envision them in the future? How might parishes be different? Are Catholic parishes in a state of evolution toward the future even now?

3. Which aspects of American religion do you find most compelling? Which do you find most unattractive or dangerous? Describe what you see as the effects in the future of these American assumptions about religion.

Chapter 5

Future Church in a Future World

Christianity has crossed many cultural boundaries that, in the past, seemed almost insurmountable. The New Testament amply documents the first, and perhaps the greatest, cultural leap: Jewish followers of Jesus encountered non-Jewish people who became committed to Christ. Initially the issue concerned non-Gentile Jews and Gentile Jews; but Christianity quickly engulfed the whole Gentile world, making its way across the Bosporus to what we now call Europe, as well as toward the Nile into Africa. Spain dates its Christian heritage from St. James, while India traces its Christian lineage to St. Thomas—both apostles of Jesus!

A quick scan of Christianity's growth shows it first with a generalized Hellenistic culture, then formally part of the Roman Empire, with vigorous churches even in North Africa. Next came the encounter with the various tribes once conquered (or nearly conquered) by the Romans, the predecessors of France, Spain, Germany, and Britain. The absorption of Christianity by these peoples took nearly half a millennium. The initial excursions into Asia, including China, left seeds of Christianity, but it never penetrated the great Eastern cultures. European Christianity then took a great leap into a vastly different world, that on the other end of the Atlantic, in the great flowerings of South and North American Christianity. This, in turn, furthered links with some parts of Asia, notably the Philippines.

But all these tremendous leaps seem to pale in comparison with the cultural leap that Christianity, in its missionary commitment, has to face at this moment in time: a modern world where secularity is the common idiom and personal choice the individual lingo. All other eras either shared the same assumptions about reality and power, or had Christians encountering a population still formally unschooled. These two factors do not exist for the Church today.

There are few common assumptions in modern life. The mains ones, however, veer toward the scientific—mathematics, physics, biology—showing its most practical side in industry and medicine. The scientific mind construes itself, almost by definition, as not needing a divine being. While many scientists do hold to the existence of God, none of them needs God in their laboratories, atom smashers, or emergency rooms. Observable reality seems to explain itself; what it cannot explain is outside of (and irrelevant to?) the domain of science. This scientific mind now extends to broad patches of modern culture and many people figure they can get by in life without reference to anything transcendent. The Church has never faced this before. The Enlightenment, which engendered the seeds of this mentality, once influenced primarily an elite class of intellectuals; now it pervades everything.

Nor has the Church faced a society that is widely educated, well beyond the high school level, and therefore able to accept a message only after critical examination. Now college-level education appears as an option in almost all cultures. Educated humanity, furthermore, exercises itself in autonomous structures of communication that go well beyond printing and publishing. TV, video, and audio now circulate freely over an uncontrollable Internet, giving every human potential exposure to an array of uncontrollable ideas.

Faith today is tested by modernity and post-modernity. If the modern tempts people today with a sense that everything can be explained in terms of scientific knowledge or research, the post-modern tempts people with the idea that most of this pursuit of truth is pointless. This double legacy derives, perhaps, from the colossal nihilism of the twentieth century, with its global wars on a scope unimaginable before. However derived, assumptions today make it difficult to sustain any inherent human meaning.

Along with secularity and education, the Church faces a world where individual choice is the prime mover of the world. This is relatively recent, as a look at our own childhoods tells us. "Little children should be seen and not heard," went one motto of my childhood. And often, children were not even seen, since parents could send them outdoors, whether in cities or in pristine suburbs, to play for hours with their friends. A highly structured authority counterbalanced this childhood freedom. Parents disciplined children without question; sometimes the parents of a friend might even discipline a child. Many Catholic children went to schools where the sway of nuns and sisters stood unquestioned. Most Catholics, and their children, went to Mass under threat of eternal damnation.

In this world, in which people matured as they graduated from high school, options were few. Before the 1950s, young adults rarely went on to college. Many married before the age of twenty. Teens saw their life-long careers well before graduation. Working in a factory, being a secretary, becoming a policeman or fireman, and perhaps a priest or a sister—these were the kinds of options that working-class Catholics thought about sixty or seventy years ago. They were options defined by a culture—a Catholicism shaped by neighborhood, clan, or small town. Was it not more like assuming a role than making a choice?

One could point to many factors that led to this world being blown apart: the building of the suburbs, the post-war G.I. bill that expanded the options for college, the Second Vatican Council, the sixties with its protests, drugs, and sex. But blown apart it was.

As a result of the nearly-global shock of the second half of the twentieth century, people grow up very differently today. Their identities are construed from a palette of choices that would have bewildered people in the first part of the twentieth-century. Biology, which controlled how maturity rolled out in a culture, plays a much smaller role; people do not have to marry in their late teens because they can control pregnancy in a variety of ways. Robert Wuthnow, in his revealing book *After the Baby Boomers,* explains that people mature and settle down almost a decade later then they did before. Since church-going strongly correlates with settling down, Wuthnow explains that millions of young adults are absent from our churches because they are involved in the long, modern process of "finding themselves."

So the world that existed in the first part of the 1900s, a world that had kinship with almost three millennia of prior culture, no longer exists. And the Church, the missionary Church, has to face this modern world, one unlike any it has faced before, as directly as our ancestors encountered Rome, or Germany, or Hispaniola, or sub-Saharan Africa.

Precisely because there is little common vocabulary, and because people have so many options (including giving up on church), the Church cannot think that repeating past approaches, or trying to replicate the past, will be effective. The Church is no longer talking to a captive audience. Our rhetoric has to be weighed by how others will be able to hear it. One can think of the past fifty years as a gradual stripping away from the American Catholic Church of those cultural elements that successfully passed on the faith from one generation to another, at least in terms of cultural patterns.

Our modern world, as we saw in chapter 2, has yielded strange fruit. One can trace meaninglessness and the crisis of community to the twin fonts of secularity and fluid personal identities. These are unresolved issues burning in the hearts of everyday Americans. This challenges faith to become a way to help modern people resolve the question of meaning in their lives. One can hide only so long from dealing with the miracle of existence itself, of the inner élan in the human heart for something more, of the need to make sense out of things, of the necessity to renew and restore relationships, of the need to overcome sin and isolation.

Our Clients

Church leaders, then, need to be quite conscious of the change in culture that has generated a very different "client" from what we had two generations ago. Secularity has given people the idea that they do not need God; the successes of secularity (technology and medicine) have spawned the added notion that people do not even need salvation. It is not uncommon, on my Facebook page, to see younger folks identify themselves as atheists, explaining, with all the wisdom of their twenty-two years, that religion was for an older, superstitious crowd.

It's tempting to address younger generations as if it were still the 1950s. How easy it is to assume that folks have to listen to us because we have the Gospel, or the infallible message, or the oldest tradition, or some endorsement from God. How simple to think we can impose the categories in which many of us were raised onto these young people who cannot possibly understand, let alone conform to, those categories.

One temptation in this context would be to dissolve all categories completely, to give the impression that anything goes because we now are liberated and "cool." Some people would claim, I feel unjustly, that this is what we did in the 1970s and 1980s. Certainly some of the American fascination with switching churches has to do with dissolving categories.

Another temptation would be to establish totally rigid categories, in order to begin fostering some kind of re-identification with the Church. Certainly a percentage of people would respond to this direction because a clear identity is something people are looking for—but it would be probably a rather small percentage. This strategy would create something like an enclave within which young people could buffer themselves from the implications of modernity and some of the extremes of experimenting involved with "finding themselves."

Neither of these approaches, tempting as they are, exactly addresses the needs of our new clients, those who were born and bred in the latter third of the twentieth century, from Gen-Xers to Millennials. The first approach only feeds into the amorphous character of modern experience. The second tries to replicate an older cultural solution that is not viable, because our contemporary culture is simply too fluid, and will remain fluid. One solution jumps into the raging stream with the very people we are trying to reach; the other tells people, as the waters are raging by, to grab onto a rock they can barely see.

Pastors, spiritual leaders, missionaries—we all simply have to contemplate more deeply the dynamics of this contemporary world. As our ancestors did before us, we have to engage and take from the world what furthers our Gospel. But because this modern world is so totally new, the engagement with it may well bring about an experience of Catholicism unlike that of previous generations. As Jesus did not dismiss anyone whose path he crossed (certainly not the various kinds of Jews he met, or even Gentiles), so modern people of mission have to engage people in the language of their modern lives. Christian (and Catholic) experience has changed over the centuries in the encounter with culture. It would be improbable for our current life not to entail changes, some of which we may not be able to clearly see.

Personal Entry Points

So what is the idiom of the world we want to touch? It has at least the following phrases in its vocabulary:

(1) *Experience* is crucial, and it is a foundation of both a scientific mentality and personal option. People will work from what is right in front of their noses. People will also absorb information from any number of sources. And people will conclude that what they experience is what is real.

(2) *Personal choice* is central. People need to be invited to make choices. Once made, those choices need to be reaffirmed again and again. The world of automatic pilot and assumed commitments no longer holds. We are closer to the more

tenuous world of the Sower and the Seed than the *Baltimore Catechism*. (See the appendix for what this parable can open for us today.)

(3) *Technology* seems to be the new *lingua franca* of today's world. People see faces; people see screens. For younger generations, these can even blend, as social networking clearly shows. People look on their electronic communities as extended families—all the better because you can delete a problem person electronically far more easily than in actual life. Technology makes community at once more accessible and more hidden.

(4) *Human contact*, and human feeling, now is universal. People can feel connected to just about anyone in the world. Culture and race need no longer be barriers; pretty soon this will be true even of languages. Feeling connected to everyone means that there is a universal sense of kinship, of interest, and even of justice. What is happening to women in Africa or Afghanistan becomes a burning issue for everyone.

(5) A consequence of this universal sense of connection is a powerful drive toward *helping others*, bettering the lives of others, being more socially committed. Young people may not agree point by point with all the tenets of Catholic social teaching, particularly those that call for a suspension of self-interest, but they will have passionate interest in helping others in direct ways. Capitalist and neo-liberal economic thrusts will remain, but these do not in themselves disqualify strong sentiments of compassion.

(6) *Personal contact* is more physical, more open, and potentially more intense. Virtually every young person we meet has a vastly different sense of sexual propriety than earlier generations. The very assumptions about sexuality are totally different in younger generations. This simply is their experience. While pastoral leaders cannot endorse most of this, neither can we be naïve about it. This means that certain moral insights will simply take longer for many people to appreciate. How sexual contact often rides along with a kind of personal anonymity as people explore each other will, I think, forever puzzle older generations.

(7) *Spirituality* remains the buzzword. It may well be impossible to know what exactly people mean by this, but it includes some sense of transcendence, of meaning, of connections to deeper things, of touching more than our palpable world. In this way, it may well be a reaction to a secularism that insists on a purely material basis for existence. We may operate as if this empiricism is the ultimate truth (particularly in the more intellectual sectors of culture), but this does not prevent people from sensing that purely material explanations simply do not provide viable answers about human life.

The Objective

Aware of the wider tensions in American society, some of which were sketched in chapters 1 and 2, and knowing the elements of the vocabulary of our new, young, world, church leaders need to be very clear about our apostolic task. More than anything else, our missionary business has to be about this one objective: **forming disciples who commit themselves to the Kingdom of God, to the mission that Jesus undertook and revealed**.

While this objective reinforces the overall thrust of speaking more in relational than in institutional terms, it also engages the elements of modern life that we sketched above. It appeals to our contemporary need for human contact and for spiritual meaning. Let me outline the basic components of discipleship which, I believe, begin to address the context of modern life: Word, community, service, and prayer.

- Discipleship, after all, presumes personal commitment and personal decision, because all our involvement with the *Word of God* forms a relationship to which people either have to open themselves or walk away. The man in the Gospels who asks about eternal life, variously described as rich or young, may not be a perfect analogue to today's world (he, at least, had enough going on to *ask* that question), but his image does show that knowing God involves a response. The Word involves us with a God to whom we must make some response. It involves, then, conversion, commitment, and perseverance.

- Discipleship also involves *community*. Despite the overall myths of American privacy and individuality, disciples do need other disciples to stay on their course, to be faithful, to persevere, to endure. Community can sometimes come in unenfleshed forms, as people decode their texts and upload their photos to Facebook. But the very connectedness of modern people brings the issue of community more easily to the forefront. Cannot young people be invited to explore how community with other disciples can become something actually experienced and sustained? Can they be invited to see community as, itself, a way to image God and God's love? Can they come to see community as a place where they can encounter God more authentically?

- Community leads to *service*, which is one of the main thrusts of the Kingdom Jesus opened for us. It involves more than a social Gospel in which all sense of union with God is subsumed into doing good. We have learned well enough in the last century that care for others must be embedded in a passionate sense of relationship with God. Jesus, after all, joined his two basic commandments, love of God and love of others. Pastoral leaders have to offer concrete roadways for people to get involved in service, in accord with their capacities. Some of that service may be within the church ambience; much of it will be beyond the parish. Some may be local; these days, some of it will be international, as disciples respond to emergencies throughout the world.

- If there is a relationship with God and others, then that has to be expressed. This is how disciples connect their personal lives with God—*through prayer*, especially with the Christian community. Disciples need to embody and enact what they believe; they need to witness to themselves and each other. Without this kind of external support, faith becomes a mental episode, bereft of the social reinforcement that is part of faith's experience. Worship, then, becomes far more than an obligation, or a routine. It becomes an encounter with God through others, embedded in the deep tradition of the Church's worship, embodied in the action of the Mass, and enhanced by the gathered community's presence.

Adopting a perspective of discipleship can help Catholics put into a fuller context the patterns we now have for transmitting faith. Much of our ministry with children and teens centers on preparing them to receive the sacraments, something essential to the pattern of their lives as Catholic disciples. But we need leverage to get beyond the limitations inherent in an overly sacrament-centered environment. We constantly hear how families come to prepare Johnnie for first Reconciliation, or Mary for Holy Communion, followed by a rather large hiatus of involvement. Then about half of those who made Holy Communion might come around for confirmation. Confirmation, as everyone acknowledges, functions like graduation, as children orbit beyond the parish's sphere of influence.

The whole process of formation in faith has to be infused with the dynamics of discipleship, not only for the children being formed but, even more, for their families. This involves helping people to gather into groups empowered to read, share, and deeply accept, the Word of God; to pray freely and fully for the accomplishment of God's will; to share opportunities and burdens; and to become agents of service and mission in the world. Parishes can come to see themselves as concentric circles of disciples, all the richer because of their Catholic heritage.

I believe that only a perspective like this can begin to touch modern people "where they live," as the slogan goes. I am arguing that adopting the structures of discipleship more fully into our everyday Catholic experience can address the profile of younger and future Catholics who grow up in today's very different world. There can be a convergence between directions that we adopt as pastors and the directions of the modern world.

Convergence

Adopting a perspective of discipleship and the Kingdom allows missionaries today to bring important lines of modern life and culture into convergence with classical Christian and Catholic themes.

The place of the Church, for instance, becomes clearer when it can be powerfully related to community, worship, and the Kingdom of God. Indeed, one of the most compelling points of invitation to the Catholic Church today is the way it so cogently reflects the dimension of the Kingdom of God, especially its universality, inclusiveness, compassion, service, and acceptance of history but with an insistence on transcendence. Too often Christianity seemed to force people into a choice between "this world" and "the world to come," as if the Incarnation had not happened. People do not have to make this kind of false choice because the Kingdom envelops all time, the present and beyond the present.

Living for the Kingdom helps people develop a fuller vision of divine life because it necessarily involves all the persons of the Trinity, helping Catholics expand their acceptance of the role of the Holy Spirit in contemporary experience. If the Eucharist is to remain central to Catholic life, it will do so by amplifying our willingness to do the will of the Father (the Kingdom *is* the Father's will), which can be done only by the power of the Holy Spirit. Eucharist, that is, leads us to involvement in the Kingdom and the Triune God of the Kingdom.

In terms of the societal factors explored in chapter 2, discipleship (especially when understood as stewardship) begins to help modern people mediate between individualism and community, between trust and hope, between the unlimited and our concrete limitations, between dreams and reality. Discipleship, hinging on the experience of death and resurrection, helps modern people let go of their need to acquire and amass because it insists that letting go lies at the heart of Christian life. **It insists on conversion, but only in relationship to others, to community and Church, and to the God of Jesus.**

Perhaps the time has come to see the Second Vatican Council not as a liberal wedge against conservatives, nor as a liberal albatross that conservatives need to get rid of, but rather as a grace-filled funnel, a conduit through time. It was the fruit of almost two centuries of rediscovering the Fathers of the Church and the way the New Testament unfolded into centuries of reflection and experience. The Council allowed Catholics in the twentieth century to go behind the way Catholicism had shaped itself after Trent and after the massive political changes that came with the emergence of democratic republics. It allowed a more catholic experience of Catholicism to emerge in the twentieth century.

After all, what we invite people to, as missionaries, is no one style of Catholicism because Catholicism is just too vast for that. We invite them to the core realities that structure Catholic belief: the Trinity, the Paschal Mystery, the Kingdom of God, the Word of God, the Church and its sacred actions, the way of discipleship, the path to holiness—a life centered on God, through Jesus and the Spirit.

Articulated in its fullness, what we Catholics have to offer amounts to a massive contribution to the way Americans see religion. American religion, as I sketched some of its elements in chapter 4, can too easily be under the sway of the more distorted parts of American life, particularly through an overemphasis on individuality and exceptionalism, and a too-ready acceptance of exploitation (because we American are "good" and "right" while everyone else is less so!).

But achieving this will demand a particular awareness of the contemporary world, at the very least so we can cogently appeal to it. Parishes can do this. Parishes can begin to address the modern crises of meaninglessness and isolation. Parishes can shift their perspective just a bit more into an emphasis on their relational and communal dimensions. I will try to point out, in chapter 6, what this might look like as a parish agenda.

As parishes do this, the future of the Church in America will come into focus. It will no longer have large ethnic parishes, convents full of nuns, children in uniform attending enormous Catholic schools, rectories full of priests trying to diversify their talents into religious education or team coaching. Catholic parishes have been slowly morphing into something new. With collaboration among clergy, lay ecclesial ministers, and laypeople of a wide array of competencies, Catholic parishes can become the nexus of the Gospel and modern American culture. America cannot easily resolve its tensions as a secular political society with religious drives. Catholic parishes, becoming an interface between immanent modern experience and a transcendence based on the Kingdom, can become communities of disciples enriched by the resources of the Church's vast tradition.

But I suspect this can only happen if parishes themselves, while engaging modern people, forthrightly see their life in more Gospel categories—as continuing the mission of Jesus, as proclaiming a change of mind and heart through the announcement of the Kingdom, as pointing to the wonders God does in our midst once we open our hearts to divine grace. This has to be what Catholics see and feel when they gather, whether for Sunday Mass or for some other ministry during the week.

Parishes will need to drink more fully of the Gospel passages they proclaim and elaborate every Sunday. Those passages amount to a charter for mission and evangelization. They call us to a more conscious and expressed appropriation of the categories of the Kingdom: mercy, grace, love, healing, community, risk, commitment, and perseverance.

Questions

1. How would you express and
   explain the main factors in the
   modern world, particularly as
   they influence the practice of
   religion? Do you personally
   see secularity growing?
   Do you think the Church is
   facing a social reality it has
   never faced before?

2. What do you think are the
   touchstones for younger
   people today in their
   personal and daily lives?
   How do believers connect
   with these touchstones?
   What are the elements of
   modern life that can speak
   to modern people?

3. Do you think that the idea
   of discipleship can prove
   fruitful for modern people?
   Do you think parishes can
   adapt a concept like discipleship for their basic approach
   to faith? What do people
   think of when they hear
   the word discipleship?

Chapter 6

An Agenda for Today's American Parish

Catholic evangelization, as articulated from our key sources—the documents of Vatican II, *On Evangelization in the Modern World, Go and Make Disciples*, and *Mission of the Redeemer*—departs in substantial ways from the individual-congregational thrust of what I've described as American religion. Nevertheless, some aspects of the American approach to religion have long fascinated Catholic leaders, particularly in terms of explicit outreach to others and use of the media. Church documents have made frequent reference to these kinds of initiatives. The idea of discipleship, as a priority of Catholic life, can also align well with dimensions of American religion. This means moving Catholics from a largely cultural approach to faith to one that is also more personal, but still communal.

So if one were to assume the priority of evangelization and discipleship, what kind of agenda does that set for American parishes today? How might a parish agenda be sketched in terms of our Catholic commitment to evangelization and our attending to the patterns that arise from modern American culture? How might Catholic parishes today orient themselves to face the modern world?

To assume these priorities of evangelization and discipleship means that a parish is committed to (1) the ongoing call to conversion of its active parishioners; (2) a consistent invitation to its less active parishioners to become more deeply involved and converted; (3) a consistent invitation to seekers to discover Jesus Christ in our Catholic tradition, and (4) the ongoing challenge for Catholics to live their faith in the midst of an increasingly secular culture.

In chapter 1, we were able to look at aspects of conversion with reference to individuals. We saw there that a notion of conversion as *identification with Jesus Christ,* in accord with the various stage of life and faith, could provide a large and comprehensive framework for thinking about what Christians have long meant by conversion. Helping Catholics see elements of conversion in their ordinary Catholic life would enormously advance their sense of being truly converted, instead of the present state, where popular ideas of conversion almost alienate Catholics and mainline believers.

Granting this, however, Catholics can still have a hard time seeing the priorities of discipleship and evangelization in their parishes. The basic agenda of parishes can become obscured by a rhythm of "automatic pilot" that highlights institutional and cultural patterns, but not those that bring discipleship into focus. In addition, Catholics in today's world are caught up in the same questions that dominate modern society, factors that spring from the dynamics of American life that we saw in chapter 2. These dynamics particularly undermine the vision of believers whose meaning comes from a profound sense of unity with God and with others in faith.

What might be some of the particular factors in today's life that parishes need to begin addressing?

Major Current Factors

American life today is driven by a crisis in community and in human meaning, both arising as a consequence of modernity. If America typifies the encounter between faith and modernity, then American society, along with Europe, has to work out the implications of secularity. A scholar like Charles Taylor, in his magisterial book *A Secular Age*, points out how reactions to what he calls the "disenchanted" universe of Enlightenment thinkers brought about a strong individuality, almost a disembedding of people from communal roots. He also notes how the modern denial of transcendence truncates our vision of human purpose and destiny. Evangelization and discipleship bring perspectives that can powerfully address this crisis.

Parishes, therefore, are responding to these distinct social factors when they seek to evangelize and call people to discipleship. People are suspended between their individuality and their need for community, between their fantasies of being unlimited and the stark limitations of their lives, between a desire for untrammeled freedom and patterns that end up enslaving them and exploiting others, between a sense of personal importance and an underlying sense of purposelessness. As the mission terrain of modern life, parishes might be uniquely poised to address these underlying issues.

The crisis in community derives from the enormous individualism and individual construction of identity that operate throughout the culture. The sense of communal cohesion, which derived so often from ethnic membership, exists today only among distinct segments of the population—notably Latinos, African-Americans, and Asian groups. Yet even in these groups communal cohesion can be quite weak, as their particular struggles, and the built-in tension between generations, make clear. The bonds people experience today are largely personal—who is connected to "me"—rather than communal. The level of mobility in modern life uproots any sense of connection with a particular geographical area. Businesses no longer have much allegiance to their employees. The rate of uncommitted sexual connection, along with the high rate of divorce, makes even the intimate connections of modern people seem fragile.

How people construct their identities today is a major complicating factor in the crisis of community. Because people have a weak sense of community, they feel, as a result, they have to hinge their unhinged lives by exploring a variety of personal identities. Our society tells people to "find themselves" by seeking new experiences; this process often begins in adolescence and ends, perhaps, in one's thirties. Because identity formation in our consumer universe is so often driven by commercial factors (what I own, what I drive, where I live, how I dress, etc.), modern people often experience an absence of a central core to themselves. We are how others perceive us; we are only a combination of certain tastes and talents. We do not feel there is much inside to hold us together.

Sin, further, brings about and intensifies our sense of isolation and our provisional identities. Sin leads us to live and act for ourselves, regardless of how that might affect another. It also undermines whatever ideals we have for ourselves, thereby distorting our self-image and identities. When we sin, we make ourselves what we cannot be, a law unto ourselves, losing fundamental perspective in the process. Sin contributes enormously to human isolation and disorientation. Even more, it creates a social environment in which our grosser, evil impulses are magnified and further influence everyone for the worse.

All of this generates, obviously, a crisis of meaning. Are we created (if we *are* created, moderns would muse) simply to make money, to have pleasure, to avoid pain, to extend life as long as possible? Are we created for any greater purpose? These deeper questions have generated a *de facto* nihilism in whole layers of the culture, demonstrated by the prevalence of depression, violence in movies, anger in music, uncommitted sexual involvement, crime, and suicide. What alternatives do people feel they have when they have been told (and are half-way convinced) that they are only the products of random combinations of atomic material at the mercy of impersonal natural forces? Like a child who is told he or she was an unplanned accident, humankind feels itself a cosmic accident.

Modern people, then, feel disconnected and meaningless.

This is what parishes have to start addressing, and an evangelizing perspective can help them do it.

Purpose and Meaning

Can faith provide, once again, a sense of purpose? We can remember the days of the *Baltimore Catechism*, when the whole purpose of life was compressed into the task of saving one's soul. The Pelagian overcast to this formulation should make all of us wince. But such a tightly-stated purpose made sense in a universe framed by terms such as law, sin, punishment, guilt, death, threat, and damnation. (While this does not describe the whole *Baltimore Catechism* era, it fairly presents a large part of its thrust.) As we have learned, over the last century, to speak of Good News, grace, faith, trust, love, openness to the Spirit, and inner peace, we have come to put these terms of judgment into better proportion; as a result, we have moved closer to the expression of faith found in the New Testament. Not that the New Testament does not have its warnings; indeed, it does. But, rather, those warnings emerge against a framework of God's gracious inbreaking into our lives.

Rick Warren's widely successful book, *The Purpose-Driven Life*, demonstrates just how much modern people long for a sense of purpose. Modernity has, wittingly or not, stripped away a sense of direction from human life, and people cannot easily live without that. Many try to find purpose in the personal realities of their lives, what we Catholics call vocation, the sense that God has a calling for every single one of us. Yet, paradoxically, just such a way of putting it this way can, in modern society, feed into the individualism that undercuts part of the broader meaning that humans need. "My vocation" can lead me to define faith as essentially individual and personal.

Catholics can restore, and put into a fuller context, this sense of purpose by reverting to the same fundamental category that Jesus used, the Kingdom, as a way to give direction to our lives. The Reign of God, which Jesus proclaimed, inaugurated, lived for, died for, and was raised for—this Kingdom is an all-consuming vision in the synoptic Gospels. It speaks powerfully of a direction for every human life, and all human history, an end state when God's mercy, justice, grace, and freedom will structure all human existence. It is predicated on a radically new relationship with God; Jesus, after all, presents the God who deserves all our heart, mind, and soul as the Father, whose gracious care is primal and abundant. Likewise, Jesus pushes the idea of love well beyond treating our neighbor as ourselves, insisting that "neighbor" is a universal category. The standard of love for a Christian is the love that Jesus himself shows. This new relationship with God and others is the foundation of the conquest of sin.

Parishes, then, can begin addressing the question of modern meaning by stating their mission this way: **we are a community that lives for the Kingdom and begins to bring the Reign of God into reality in our present existence**. Catholics find their purpose, their vocation, by being part of the community of Christ's faithful, contributing their gifts to serve the cause of God, the Kingdom.

The non-synoptic writings in the New Testament do not seem to use the category of Kingdom as clearly as the synoptic Gospels. This, however, does not mean that the category is entirely absent. Rather, it shows up in a different way—Paul, John, Peter, James, and the letter to the Hebrews explore the meaning of the Kingdom in terms of the spiritual realities of actual Christian life—community, prayer, worship, love, faith, faithfulness and, pre-eminently, the experience of the Holy Spirit. In other words, Kingdom is the dominant image, and discipleship is its correlative image.

Priorities

One further point before an agenda can be elaborated: pastors have to start putting first what is first. People have to see, feel, and know what comes first immediately and instinctively. And what comes first is not the institution, or the particular needs of the institution. This, however, is what Catholics often see. We keep focusing on the parish as an institution that has to be kept up, demanding that parishioners fulfill their responsibilities in this upkeep.

The problem with this is clear—people think their faith is all about a thing, or about things, for which they have to contribute or raise money. Of course the Church has an institutional, visible element to it; no one can question that. Jesus had a human body, formed a community of followers, and sent them on a mission. People contributed, women helped (as they still do!), and Judas kept the purse.

But what people need to see more clearly is this: the purpose of any church institution is the Kingdom of God, understood as God's sweeping vision of renewal for humankind. People need to experience the truth that relationship speaks far more powerfully, and truthfully, about the meaning of Catholicism than institution does. We are in an era when our institutions are undergoing radical change, parishes are closing or merging, and Catholic schools are shrinking in a substantial way. Catholics, clergy and lay, shudder at what is happening. But this very institutional contraction might be the greatest opportunity for us—to begin pointing more clearly to what our parishes are all about.

Our agenda as Catholic parishes, sharing in the bishop's mandate of mission, is clear. We are to proclaim the Kingdom and perform the deeds, under the Spirit's power and direction, that demonstrate its presence and cogency in the lives of people. All structure in the Church, whether corporate or material, exists to further our relationship with the God of Jesus and our involvement in the attitudes and actions of the Kingdom. Corporate structures such as hierarchy, ministers, and ministries, serve the Kingdom—and they will be judged by it. Material structure like money, buildings, and allocation of resources, serve the Kingdom—and our uses of them will be judged by it.

Pastors will develop an effective agenda for today when they stop presenting the needs of the institution ahead of everything else. Instead, pastors have to more clearly relate those needs to the Kingdom of God.

I can now begin to draw up an agenda for parish. The agenda items are not organized in chronological order or by absolute priority; rather, they follow from issues of meaning and community that we have identified as the crucial cultural factors that bear upon faith life today. They constitute the seeds of an evangelizing parish plan for today's world.

The Agenda

- **Parishes must help people use the meaning of faith to forge identities centered on Jesus Christ.**

"I no longer live, but Christ lives in me," was how St. Paul put it (Galatians 2:20), showing a radical identity in Christ—both Christ individually and Christ in his corporate body, the Church. This radical identity means both the commitment to renounce sin and the accepted purpose to live for the cause of God.

The Word of God asks for a response; consistent response begins to shape identity. Catholic life means ongoing conversion; ongoing conversion means putting the Kingdom of God at the center of one's life and making decisions in terms of it. Catholics desperately need a sense of conversion—not something alien that does not correspond to our tradition, but a deeper appropriation of the force of our tradition as it calls us to reaffirm Jesus Christ and live in Christ's Spirit.

When people experience something deeper, as the result of a retreat or other religious experience, they often cannot put their finger on what it was. Somehow the same Mass, the same sermon, the same Bible class, all of a sudden become crucial and involving. The change occurred in the individual, in his or her identity with Christ through the particular bonding that happened among a group of people who have consciously begun to see themselves as disciples.

Parishes actually have many resources to make this happen, but they are often not followed up or coordinated. Catholics will, for example, show up for sacramental preparation, and this can be linked far more clearly to discipleship and ongoing formation than usually happens. Parishes will often invite a special preacher into the parish, but the preparation and follow-up to this special event often goes by the wayside. Parishes, too, often get connected to retreat houses or spiritual movements, but the sense of retreat usually stays with a smaller group and not the whole congregation. Every Eucharist, when celebrated with deliberation and fervor, actually involves parishioners in this dynamic of identifying with Christ. All parish ministries are resources for a deeper experience of identifying with Jesus.

Proclamation of meaning in Jesus Christ involves, of course, proclamation of the Kingdom of God, with its powerful notes of mercy, love, healing, restoration, relationship, discipleship, and service. The more parishes, in their activities, look like Jesus in his actions, the more they will be able to speak to people in compelling ways. Pastoral leaders can well reorient and refresh themselves in their work by frequently reading the first two chapters of the Gospel according to Mark.

As we are so often well reminded, the adult Catechumenate is an excellent image of how faith can be communicated among people in an open and accepting setting. That should be a big clue for parishes today—how to structure their adult faith formation programs, youth groups, young adult ministries, small groups, senior ministry, and other formation ministries of the parish.

People pick and choose the parts of their identities today, often well into their forties; parishes need to give people a reason to want to pick faith as a key part of their personal identities. We have to be about the business of helping people find their meaning in the mystery of Jesus.

- **Parishes have to help their parishioners situate their spirituality in the framework of the vision of Jesus— that is, the Trinity—with particular emphasis on the Holy Spirit.**

Catholics can be almost totally innocent (ignorant?) of the place of the Holy Spirit in their lives. On the one hand, Catholics are enormously Christocentric because Jesus is, obviously, the revelation of God in human terms. This Christocentrism only gets reinforced by Catholics' almost exclusive focus on the Holy Eucharist.

On the other hand, Jesus cannot be understood or appropriated in the lives of believers without a strong emphasis also on the Holy Spirit. After all, Jesus died, rose, and ascended into heaven (that is, took possession of the Kingdom) precisely to send the Holy Spirit upon his followers. It is the Holy Spirit who creates the dynamic of Christian life whereby believers "put on the Lord Jesus Christ," which means undertaking his mission, absorbing his values, exercising his deeds of compassion and mercy, praying with complete openness to the Father, and trusting with complete fidelity through life and death. This is what it means to identify with Christ Jesus.

A renewed sense of the Holy Spirit might get Catholics out of their default modes (safe, quiet, inward-looking and, yes, automatic pilot) into those modes that better characterize Christian life. A parish that is not emphasizing the Holy Spirit in ways accessible to its parishioners is a parish only partially fulfilling its mission. While the Church has much reason to thank the Charismatic Renewal for its consciousness of the Spirit, it can hardly depend on purely Charismatic modes of operation to help parishioners grasp the Holy Spirit. The Spirit is as present in mysticism, contemplation, social action, daily prayer, and ordinary life as it is in extraordinary manifestations of signs and wonders. We need to start pointing to this.

- **Parishes have to realize they have a precious, relevant, and powerful message to share with parishioners and the world. They cannot shortchange the liturgy of the Word, and the ministries of the Word that flow from it.**

Preaching and catechesis have the ability to speak to the very issue of meaninglessness. They can emphasize a God who gives meaning to all existence because divine love grounds both creation and its fulfillment, and because an intensely personal God, who is pure relationship in the Trinity, grounds all human relationships. The coming, death, resurrection, and ascension of Jesus Christ are God's affirmation of human being and human meaning. Teaching Christ, pastors must point to the emptiness of modern myths that paint images of mindless forces and random combinations of atoms, as if that could begin to explain human experience. To deal with today's sense of meaninglessness, Catholics can present the rich troves of our theology and spirituality in a way that can be heard, absorbed, and developed by modern people.

Catholics can get motivated to plumb their faith more deeply and, more importantly, apply faith teachings to their individual lives, only if they are hearing a powerful message that begins when they worship. How the Lectionary selections are proclaimed, how that proclamation is nestled in the prayer and music that frame it, and how the Scriptures are given a living edge by preachers: this is the fount out of which any other growth in the Word of God will take place.

Adult faith formation has been in crisis since the 1960s. On the one hand, certain Catholics argue that parishioners do not understand the teaching of the Church; they see information about Catholic teaching as indispensible. On the other hand, many Catholics vote with their feet when offered adult religious education, finding the content not relevant to their individual concerns.

Understanding faith certainly has to go beyond reading or memorizing parts of the Catechism. The Catechism sees itself as a resource book, not a direct conduit to the life of Catholics. Other resources, however, are constantly appearing; the Catholic book publishing industry (however much is left of it, given today's changes) produces scads of informative and inspiring books each year. But information needs a context: that of Catholics identifying with Christ through the Word. Until we are consistently opening the Word of God in relevant ways to our people, no adult appropriation of faith is likely.

All the exciting, and promising, directions in catechetics today involve a dialogical reception of the Word of God. Parishes that have been able to sustain intergenerational approaches to catechesis report both great reception to this process and great success. Religion teachers almost universally acknowledge a need to get away from a classroom model of teaching faith, precisely as a way to engender and maintain a powerful sense of discipleship among the young. We have the beginnings of an answer, but we do not have the answer yet.

- **Parishes have to discover the power of the Eucharist to draw people into discipleship.**

As we saw in chapter 4, the Mass, which Catholics consider their greatest asset, does not get widespread endorsement from the wider American society. If people "vote with their feet," they have voted more against the Mass than in its favor. Fewer people attend Mass consistently; more people today decide to explore their faith in a non-Mass setting. This, of course, seems incomprehensible to a Catholic who rightly grasps the Mass as God's definitive sign of presence in our midst, in Jesus through the Spirit. What seems definitive for us, however, seems quite dispensable for many Catholics and non-Catholics.

Can it be that the experiential side of the Mass is not reaching people today? If this is the case, we can point to several clear reasons: (1) the perfunctory, and sometimes cavalier, way ministers celebrate their various ministries in the Mass; (2) the anonymous way Catholics often gather for worship, without strong connection with their fellow Catholics; (3) the tendency to look at the Mass as a sequence people go through rather than an expression of their deepest relationship with God. In the Eucharist, the incarnational dimension of God's relationship to humankind appears once again: in the concrete, in the human, God is made palpable.

Many times the issues about Mass seem to set the "vertical" against the "horizontal," the transcendent dimension of Mass, which is God-focused, versus the communal dynamics of the participants. The problem, of course, is that both these dimensions get shortchanged by parishes. The reality of God's presence in Jesus and the Spirit at Eucharist relates directly to the presence parishioners experience with each other. People will not arrive at a high sense of the presence of God unless this is reinforced in the ways Catholics relate to each other and to God.

I often get the feeling that reverence, for some people, means a kind of abstraction, a removal from present space and time. Were that true, the Incarnation would make no sense. Reverence has to be the way created reality becomes centered on God with (as the Scriptures put it) all its heart, soul, mind, and strength. Our practice of reserving the Eucharist is a way of extending over time the action of the Mass. Note, however, that we reserve the consecrated bread both for adoration and also for support of the sick and dying. The Lord continually calls us inward, in reflection, and outward, in service. Affirming the real presence, in the consecrated species with its attendant doctrines, will not bring passionate reverence about by itself; it has to be reinforced, today, by a personal experience of real presence in community.

When Eucharist is felt as profound prayer, communal prayer, interactive prayer, dynamic prayer—something that all ministers from priest to usher can communicate—then the potential of the Mass to be an evangelizing event, one that gathers ever more people into ever deeper connection with God and each other, will begin to be realized. The days of attending Mass out of obligation have long passed. If not obligation, then what will it be? This: powerful connection, without which belief cannot thrive.

- **Parishes need to lead their people into more consistent, daily prayer.**

Catholic life should be one of instinctual prayer. We see evidence of this through centuries of Catholic life. Some of that prayer was more formal and structured, and some of it informal.

The changes that came about after the Second Vatican Council did not always serve the purposes of daily prayer. On the one hand, the attitude was to urge Catholics to get beyond a sense of obligation and external recitation to something more personal and involving. On the other hand, many of the structured forms of prayer lost their place in Catholic life. To be sure, some of this effort had important purposes, particularly the drive to help Catholics read and be more familiar with the Bible. Needless to say, getting Catholics more comfortable with the Bible still has a way to go, even though a lot has been accomplished. Nevertheless, a vacuum exists in the lives of many Catholics: that of consistent, daily prayer.

This is why parishes need to help Catholics develop a daily discipline of prayer, touching the key points in everyday life, and expressing a broad spirituality that gives Catholics access to the fullest relationship with the Triune God, to the richest expression of holiness, and to the greatest range of spiritualities. Prayer involving all the persons of the Trinity, with the distinct spirituality each evokes, and prayer that spans personal and communal, the contemplative and the more active, all have a place in Catholic prayer life. The Catholic tradition of making the various parts of the day sacred through prayer needs to be revived in new and viable ways today.

Through bulletins, retreats, workshops, and parts of homilies, parishes have to help Catholics make prayer regular, personal, and fruitful in their lives. References to Scripture, examples of prayer, outlines of meditations, discussions of contemplation, prayerful paths through various scriptural books: all need to become part of what goes into our bulletins. Part of the benefit of small-group sharing consists in undergirding just this kind of system of daily prayer, for individuals, families, and different gatherings of believers.

- **Parishes need to be dynamic centers of community; this means not only welcoming people, but helping people connect with each other with an open sense of acceptance and access.**

More parishes are doing the externals of welcoming people; one sees this as a regular feature in the South and West, and a growing feature in the rest of the country, particularly the suburbs. The welcome sometimes only extends to saying "hello" to parishioners as they come through the door, which, to be sure, is better than nothing. But it does not often permeate the worship zone itself, as parishioners can be rather oblivious of each other.

A further sense of community needs to come about by helping parishioners associate with each other, creating bonds that personalize the large gathering of parish. Most observers of parish life note that the larger congregation usually is broken down into smaller groupings. Often, however, this sense of connection does not extend much beyond the 10 to 15 percent of people who are regularly involved in the parish's ministry. What mega-churches teach us is the need people have to aggregate in small groups of one sort or another. In addition, they teach us that people in the large congregation, on Sunday, cannot be in anonymous relationships with the parishioners who surround them and are joining them in worship. People need to *feel* community today. It cannot be presumed.

More subtle yet is the difficulty that parishioners might have in feeling a sense of access to the parish and its ministries. Often an inner circle calls the shots, not only in the parish but even more in the various ministry groups of the parish. If this is what parishioners feel, imagine what visitors to the parish might feel! Creating a sense where everyone feels encouraged to participate in ministry needs to overcome attitudinal barriers in many parishes.

Pastors need to sit down with all their advisory groups and talk frankly about the "affect" that parishioners radiate and how to move it more in the direction of making community more central in the ethos of the parish. Explicit emphasis on having people introduce themselves at meetings, and recognizing visitors in the congregation, cannot be overemphasized.

- **Parishes need to have ongoing small groups meeting at every level of parish life.**

Almost all parishes that have viable small-group sharing seem successful. Forming small groups can accomplish two goals: community and an increased consciousness of faith. Catholics cannot feel like disciples unless they are talking and sharing with others—at the very least, with each other. Pastors need to empower parishioners in a positive way to appropriate their faith, without intimidating them and driving them back into the shells where Catholics love to hide. A sense that people can read the Scriptures, or some article, and grow by discussing this with others can come to permeate the life of the congregation. For many, this will appear as a powerful new experience of the Church.

Sharing has to happen in groups of teens, young adults, parents, business people, empty nesters, stay-at-home-parents, seniors, and the various ministry segments of the parish. Some parishes successfully have every group that meets during the week share about the upcoming Sunday reading at the beginning of its meeting. The groups report a dramatic improvement in the quality of the meetings.

Sometimes small groups can become little clubs, with rather exclusive and inward-looking attitudes. Pastors need to help these groups see their need to be open to newcomers, to be welcoming and to reach out; they also need to appreciate their potential dynamic quality—that people will want to change groups or move to different kinds of groups as they get involved in the parish.

Attention to small group leaders, needless to say, is a *sine qua non* of this ministry.

- **Parishes need to see their own "registered" member- ship as a direct object of evangelization and invita- tion.**

Pastors presume that everyone is in the loop, forgetting that they know a lot of things that hardly anyone else knows, and that they have a sense of the parish that passes over the heads of most of their congregants. Parish leaders also are becoming increasingly more aware that a smaller percentage of their parishioners consistently attend church, and a grow- ing number, for a variety of reasons, attend less consistently. If getting the attention of those who come on Sunday is notoriously difficult, imagine how off the radar screen our parish looks to those who don't come, even many registered parishioners.

So registered parishioners no longer form the in group; we can't pre- sume they are present and involved. Rather, the parish roster serves as a more particularly defined picture of the wider evangelization issues that affect most of society, the casual place of religion in the lives of modern people. If pastors are not consistently inviting *all their own parishioners* to faith and deeper involvement, they are not even getting to first base in terms of the issues parishes face today.

Families with children should be one basic target of this outreach to one's own parishioners. How faith thrives in Catholic family life today is unclear to many. The older forms of Catholic school and parish-centered social activities have come under increasing pressure because of the mo- bility and diversity of modern life. Parents sincerely want to raise their children as Catholics; they know there has to be a more explicit exercise of faith, in its various dimensions, in the home. But they do not know con- cretely how to do this. They need, and want, to be reached.

Suggestions for family prayer, family social-service involvement, and family support structures (notably, parents talking with other parents) can begin to bring definition to this issue for parents today. Suggestions for intergenerational activities in the home, including even grandparents, might go far. The old bromide, "Catholic parents are the prime educators of their children," was hardly credible fifty years ago; we all knew that the parochial school was the prime educator, and priests back then had no problem telling parents they were going to hell for not using the parochial school system. It is more credible today: parents need to be realistically empowered to be the prime educators (meaning evangelizers) of their children.

Family outreach should not obscure the need to touch other demographic segments of the parish. Young adults attend church in notoriously low percentages. They need something like their own turf to establish a viable identity in the parish. Parishes often have a youth minister; one of this minister's primary roles is helping teens reach other teens. Emptynesters are a growing category in contemporary life; these folks often will respond to an invitation to be ministers. Seniors, to be sure, attend church with more regularity than any other age group; but they know friends who still await reconciliation with God.

So how do parishes begin to reach out as missionaries to their own registered members? Bulletins are minimally helpful, but they clearly are not the answer. Most bulletin material is the babble of the inner group. Bulletins do not usually engage people in their reflective and decision-making lives. So this has to happen apart from the bulletin. Periodic, but regular, communications to parishioners around issues of faith and discipleship, in whatever form makes sense, should move up high on a parish's agenda. I suggest doing this five or six times a year. These messages cannot just be about money or the bishop's appeal; they have to be about faith and the issues of faith today. Even if most parishioners do not read these communications in detail, a pastor has at least made a connection with people who tend to be disconnected in modern life. Not everything needs to be handled by letter. Innovative use of e-mail and web pages will be more and more necessary. Perhaps short videos on topics can be produced and sent out. Whatever the case or method, pastors need to address their parishioners consistently about living their faith today in positive ways (without scolding them!).

- **Parishes have to consistently reach out to those who have no faith or who have ceased participating in faith communities.**

Nothing characterized the life of Jesus so much as reaching out, particularly to those who did not belong religiously, to those who were often dismissed by the established religious leaders.

By reaching beyond their own membership, to those who have no church or who are not active in the practice of their faith, parishes can demonstrate the power of our gospel message, bring new energy to our parish communities, and help parishes break free of the mostly inward vision that often characterizes them. To the extent that parishes have taken seriously their crucial role in helping people deal with contemporary issues of meaninglessness and disconnection, to that extent people who are not members of the Church will be drawn to it.

At the very least, parishes need to consistently invite seekers and Catholics who have become absent, in order to invite them to the richer life of discipleship. The purpose of this is not merely to increase attendance at church. Rather, our very love for others, and our desire to extend the fullness of discipleship (grace, forgiveness, mercy, service, union with God) demand that we reach beyond our own circle of parishioners. To be effective, a parish's outreach has to be more than occasional, sporadic efforts. People need to know throughout the year that the parish is prepared to welcome them. Empowering an evangelization team with a focus on "who is not here" can greatly help a parish keep its focus outward as well as inward.

Perhaps pastors and parishioners fear that such outreach might lead to neglect of active parishioners. But this ignores the fact that if a parish is not reaching out, is not giving its parishioners a consistent image of Catholic life as sharing and gift, the parish is *already* being neglected, and being neglected in an essential way. **A parish not fulfilling its missionary mandate has only a truncated experience of parish.**

Whether they use programs developed by special evangelization ministries or create their own forms of outreach, parishes that undertake outreach beyond the comfort of their own regular members, in my experience, will feel enormous energy and a renewed sense of purpose among the active members of the parish. Parishioners like the idea that their parish is reaching out in mission.

We have to remind ourselves all the time that the purpose of parish lies outside itself, in the way it demonstrates the Kingdom to others and the way it invites others to participation in the Kingdom. Parishes do not exist for themselves. They exist for the world—the wider assemblies of people whom parishioners are called to serve

- **Parishes must be about serving others, particularly the poor and frail, as much as they are about the rest of their business.**

What do parishioners see when they come to their parish? The range of things might be quite impressive, from Scripture study to sacramental preparation, from ministry formation to the education of children, from small groups to various social gatherings.

What parishes do not see so much of, however, is powerful, direct, and consistent outreach to the poor and socially marginal, particularly to non-parishioners. Yet this is exactly what the people around Jesus saw him doing, reaching those who were unreached by the religious structures of his day. In fact, Jesus used precisely these kinds of actions to demonstrate the inbreaking of the Kingdom of God. One cannot read the Gospel according to Mark or Luke without an astonishing sense of just this pastoral service that constituted the Kingdom-agenda of Jesus. Even the seemingly more esoteric Gospel according to John is structured around those signs of compassion and healing that revealed the nature of Jesus and the purpose of his life. One might even argue, with complete theological integrity, that the death of Jesus was the ultimate act of service, the "finished" sign that revealed the heart of God.

Dramatic signs of God's Reign also involve healing and forgiveness. Parishes can use both the sacrament of healing, offered in a communal setting on a regular basis, and non-sacramental prayer for healing to demonstrate the compassionate connection so many people long for today. Likewise, the powerful exercise of the Sacrament of Reconciliation, both individually and communally, and an accepting attitude shown to everyone, can give evidence of the liberation Jesus promised those who opened their hearts to the Kingdom.

Many parishes, to be sure, have social action or justice commissions, or St. Vincent de Paul societies. But these hardly penetrate the consciousness of a parish; and they should. Parishes have barely begun to stretch their legs when it comes to service, to doing what Jesus did in the categories of today. When every capable parishioner sees herself or himself called to service and involved in it, then the power of the Kingdom will begin to dawn on us and the world. When people see our parishes as centers of reconciliation and peace, rather than bastions of self-protection, the latent power of our Church will be more evident. We need a lot more of the "finger of God," driving out the demons, whether physical or spiritual, that compromise so much of life in order to point the way to God's Kingdom in our midst.

Summing Up: The Near and the Far

What evolved as the ethos of American Catholicism between the 1880s and the 1950s is either under siege or disappearing. Our primarily cultural methods of passing faith from one generation to another have been disrupted by the entirely new ways in which modern people grow up, think, decide, and live their lives. The invention of the suburb and modern styles of growing up have made a return to the 1950s impossible.

So there is both an immediate agenda for evangelization, in response to the current crises of community and meaninglessness, and a long-term agenda, which involves the development of a new ethos, a new method of living and passing on faith. It will take many decades to sort out what this means and what Catholicism will look like in half a century. Look how long it took to fix a distinct pattern in American Catholicism in the nineteenth and early twentieth centuries.

Nevertheless this longer-term evolution of Catholic faith has been underway for some few decades now and its final shape has not yet been determined. Our ongoing experience of modern American culture, and the ways that what I've called American religion respond to it (adequately and inadequately) give some signposts into the future. The elements of a parish agenda for today are an attempt to make the broader patterns clearer and more accessible for Catholic leaders today. Catholics have been equipped by the Holy Spirit to deal powerfully with the malaise that emerges from modern life, from a growing secularity. As parishes awaken the capacities that the Spirit bestows on us, as they engage in the truly creative period of grounding faith in today's culture, they will then not only be fulfilling their proper role, but, even more, shaping what Catholicism will look like in America for the rest of the twenty-first century.

Questions

1. How would you identify the basic mission challenge to your parish today? What are the concrete circumstances and challenges to which your parish is trying to respond? How can your parish keep "those not here" in its focus?

2. How do you think your parish can engage more effectively with today's world? How would this be shown in the particular situation of your parish?

3. Look ahead ten years. What do you see for your parish? What kinds of growth seem possible? What might a more missionary perspective bring to your parish's future? What agenda will you develop to help your parish evangelize more effectively?

Appendix
A New Testament Spirituality for Mission

This appendix serves as a resource for the preceding chapters. It offers a way for readers to reflect on the New Testament in light of the way it calls believers to mission, to reaching out in faith. Each section can be explored by itself; readers may return to some sections several times. The mission perspective among the earliest followers of Jesus, amply present in every part of the New Testament, stands as a perpetual witness to all generations of Christians and Catholics—to embody their spirit, and spirituality, in our own personal and pastoral lives.

Why did the story of the Sower and the Seed come to be at the top of the parables of Jesus collected by St. Mark and St. Matthew? Because in some way, this parable spoke to the lived experience of the first followers of Jesus—experiences of mission and its consequences. For this reason, it can speak to us today.

Several things stand out in the parable. First, one notices that the seed is widely scattered. The sower does not carefully put one seed into the ground, then measure off a particular distance and place a second seed. The seed, rather, appears to be thrown around, as if there is an excess of abundance. In this way, the seed represents the abundant power, and sheer generosity, of God in revealing Good News through Jesus.

One also notices that the process of sowing is not uniform. Not all the seed bears fruit; nor will all the seed bear equal fruit. This shows us that early Christian experience hardly appears to have been an unmitigated success. It was fraught with the prospect of failure. Rather than being a modern marketing experience of inevitable success, the parable shows a rather sober realization of what it is like to proclaim God's Word: hits and misses.

One notices, too, *why* the seed doesn't take root. Some of it falls on shallow ground, and cannot put down roots. Some of it falls amid thorny bushes where the thorns choke it off. Some seed does not even get a chance to grow; birds eat it as soon as it falls. These images can be elaborated in a variety of ways, of course. The extension of this parable in the Gospels (Mark 4:14-20; Matthew 13:18-24) gives us a peek at what was happening in the early Church.

The seed on the path represents people who hear the "word of the kingdom without understanding it"; the evil one steals what was sown in the heart of the person. The seed on rocky ground represents those whose faith does not develop because of tribulation or trial. In other words, the Word was accepted and understood, but fear caused people to give up their faith. The seed fallen among the thorns represents yet a different threat to discipleship. The thorns do not represent persecution; rather, they represent "worldly anxiety and the lure of riches." This undoubtedly meant for early Christians, at least in part, rejecting a life of charitable love (as Matthew 25 reveals). The early Christians, then, saw their community under constant assault. They experienced people accepting, and then falling away from, the Gospel. Yet none of that blunted their sense of having to spread the seed, to proclaim God's Word. Indeed, the experience of seeing others fall away appears to have given them even greater incentive to share the Gospel with others.

How do the categories of this parable play out in our own lives today? People's growth in discipleship can often be stunted and even destroyed—can we have a better image for thinking about what Catholics go through from adolescence to young adulthood? The seed on rocky ground: we have modern comparisons for this in people who are evangelized but not catechized, or, on the other hand, catechized but not evangelized. For those who stop growing because of fear, a comparable in modern life would be the shame people might feel in being identified as believers or active churchgoers when their peers disparage them. This would seem a particular threat to the young today, who are so prone to peer pressure. The thorns, for us moderns, represent how we often worry far more about our investments and possessions than about people living right next door to us. Shallowness, fear, and comfort play out in a host of ways in modern American life.

This first parable, then, helps give us a context for mission and evangelization today: the hard work of sowing seed and seeing few results is offset by the consolation of the abundance of the seed. God's Word, in Jesus, has a power of itself; it produces even in the face of disappointment and failure. It calls us to have constant recourse to the Word of God, and to be indefatigable in sharing it. It produces and yields thirty or sixty or even a hundredfold, all in proportion to how deeply it is received.

The energy, the profligacy if you will, of the sower, calls out to us. Why does he want to sow? Why does he continue sowing? What does he know about how crucial God's Word is to the work he does? Mission arises from just this sense of overwhelming grace, of the boundless gifts of God given us in Jesus and the Spirit. Once we have received that, once the seed has borne fruit in us, then its dynamic is to bear fruit again, through us, in others.

In the face of this kind of realistic view of success and failure in spreading God's Word, what might be some fundamental spiritual insights needed to sustain mission? Among those I can list: the Paschal Mystery, the sense of being sent, the virtues of humility and confidence, the role of the Kingdom of God, and openness to the Holy Spirit. These seem to me to be a solid foundation for a biblical spirituality for evangelization.

The Paschal Mystery of Jesus

Entry into the Kingdom happens through radically identifying with Jesus Christ. This identification occurs most explicitly in the process of death and resurrection, which is the fundamental pattern of Christian life. This pattern works itself out on various levels (sacramental, emotional, vocational, biographical, even parochial); but spiritually Catholics are challenged to make this pattern the conscious focus of their lives.

The process of death and resurrection brings into sharp focus Jesus' teaching about the Kingdom, for it raises the fundamental issue of trust. Everything about human nature resists death—rightly so, because death appears as ultimate destruction of human existence. If we must experience death, however, how will we do that? Can we so trust in God that we place even our death in the divine hands? Can we so trust in God that we are free to live for God's values, for the cause that Jesus revealed? Can we so trust in God that we are willing to relinquish what must die in our lives in order to accept Jesus' Spirit and be transformed? We stand suspended between two of sayings attributed to Jesus on the Cross: "My God, why have you abandoned me?" and "Father, into your hands I entrust my spirit." Our spiritual lives are a process of navigating between these two moments.

Baptism might give us the sense that death and resurrection has already happened. We read Romans 6:3-11 at the Easter Vigil, when the elect are baptized, and we echo the themes of this passage in every baptism. Certainly, in one sense death and resurrection happen in Baptism, because we are taken from the realm of darkness and accepted into the kingdom of light. But, in an even more profound sense, death and resurrection occur in Baptism *as a pattern for the rest of our existence*. The core of Baptism has to be elaborated in the unfolding of our lives.

Looked at this way, much of Catholic ministry is helping people celebrate death and resurrection in their lives—to see, accept, and live these patterns as they unfold in a person's life story. Certainly, every time we celebrate the Mass, we re-enact our commitment to this pattern. We make the self-gift of Christ, in his death, the gift of ourselves. If we are honest, we have to recognize that we accept this Paschal pattern reluctantly. If we are honest, we have to acknowledge that modern people follow other patterns—getting ahead, proving themselves, being acknowledged, making money and, at the least, avoiding pain—much more readily, and that we ourselves often behave just like all other modern people.

When we look, however, at the fundamental values of Catholicism, the only real pattern for human existence is the one Jesus showed us. As a result, spiritual discipline has to mean turning our hearts more consistently toward this basic Paschal pattern, and slowly extirpating from our lives alternative patterns.

The temptation today, of course, is to emphasize only one or another part of the Paschal Mystery. Some of us tend to want only resurrection, without a clue as to how resurrection comes about. We want consolation, joy, peace, and sometimes even riches, because Jesus is raised. We think we can ignore the prayer attributed to St. Francis, which so cogently tells us that it's only by dying that we have eternal life. Was that not one of the temptations of some early Christians, to believe that the resurrection had already happened? (See 2 Timothy 2:18.) Maybe, in a different form, it is ours as well. Others of us emphasize the death side of the Paschal Mystery, making Christian life into duty, pain, struggle, shame and scrupulosity. For centuries we hoisted the crown of thorns onto people's heads and spoke mostly of self-castigation. In this way, we distorted the full message of Christianity.

A mature spirituality sees both dimensions at work, often paradoxically at the same time, with death and resurrection occurring in reciprocal and surprising ways. Even Jesus had to insist (in the face of obvious resistance) that his disciples had to take up their cross daily; if they refuse, then discipleship is impossible (Luke 14:26-27). Paul's experience was exactly this: "For we who live are constantly being given up to death for the sake of Jesus, so that the life of Jesus may be manifest in our mortal flesh" (2 Corinthians 4:11).

Being Sent, Going Forth

Once I know that the basic Christian pattern is that of letting go in trust, I can then be open to other dimensions of evangelization.

While we almost automatically think of Christian life as being "called," we cannot read the Scriptures without grasping that virtually everyone who is called is also sent. This might not seem immediately obvious. We are struck by the way the Gospel according to Mark develops, with the often-repeated command of Jesus that no one be told of a healing; that seems to be the opposite of being sent. It seems more like keeping quiet about the Gospel. This, however, is Mark's way of waiting until Jesus unveils his own identity as the Christ, one chosen and anointed to suffer rejection and death (Mark 8:29). Once it is clear what being "the Christ" means, the need for secrecy vanishes; then the Word can go forth, and people can bring it!

The strange story of the Gerasene demoniac in Luke (8:26-39) provides a keen comment on being sent. This man, possessed by demons, approaches Jesus in pagan territory as Jesus arrives by boat; Jesus drives the demons out and sends them into a herd of swine. The man, now in his right mind and clothed, begs to remain with Jesus, but Jesus says, "Return home and recount what God has done for you." Indeed, the man goes off and proclaims "throughout the whole town" what God has done for him in Jesus. Being sent, then, can mean several things. Every Christian, at the very least, is sent among his own, to proclaim what God has done.

In fact, whenever something great has happened to us, we cannot keep our mouths shut!

In every strata of the New Testament one finds the idea of sending. In the Gospel according to Matthew, Mark, and Luke, this is primarily found among the Apostles, but is not limited to them. With Mark, when Jesus initially calls the Twelve, it was "so he might send them forth to preach" (Mark 3:14). Mark then shows Jesus sending the Twelve again (6:6b-13), which is reported by Matthew and Luke as well. But Luke has a *further* sending, this time of seventy-two other disciples (Luke 10:1-12), which is very telling. The number seventy-two is clearly symbolic, just like the number twelve. If twelve represents the tribes of Israel, seventy-two represents the number of Gentile nations that the Jews counted. Jesus is sending his message to the world.

Paul frequently designates himself an Apostle, that is, as one who is sent. But Paul functions as the center of a large missionary enterprise involving many other men and women. He frequently alludes to this network at the beginning and end of his letters. The names Timothy and Titus stand out among those Paul sent as delegates; likewise the names Phoebe and Lydia represent people who helped Paul organize Christian communities as part of his mission. Luke, who also wrote the book of Acts, organizes the many narratives he collects around major missionary figures, notably Peter, Stephen, Philip, and Paul. The mission journeys and messages in Acts make our minds dizzy with all the movement and action.

Even in the Gospel according to John, which many people read as if it were an almost monk-like, passive Gospel, is filled with the sense of being sent. John's major stories encapsulate missionary ventures to the Samaritans, the poorer Jews (such as the man born blind) and more established Jews (Martha, Mary and Lazarus). Symbolically, John has three different signs of abundance, all indicating great missionary fruit: the water changed to wine, the distribution of the bread, and the catching of the fish at the end of the Gospel. Very pointedly, Jesus, on his first appearance to his disciples after his resurrection, says to them, "As the Father has sent me, so I send you" (John 20:21). Just as Jesus understood himself as being sent by the Father, so now he imparts that same mission to his disciples.

Catholics today, by and large, do not have a sense that they are sent on mission. They still hold a perspective that encourages them to keep what they have, to protect it and build it up for themselves. So while we Catholics readily make sense of growing in faith, or growing spiritually, or keeping the faith, we have a difficult time thinking of ourselves as being sent into the world. This is despite the fact that, at the end of every Mass, we are being commissioned in the dismissal rite to bring our faith to the world. Whether accurate or not, my sense is that since the millennium we Catholics have been more circling the wagons than acting like pioneers.

Pastoral leaders and preachers have to help Catholics flesh out this sense of being sent. Certainly, few of us are called to foreign lands, and few, too, to direct apostolic or pastoral ministry as clergy or lay ecclesial ministers. But all are sent out to the cluster of worlds that constitutes their daily experience, particularly the world of their households, friends, neighbors, and coworkers. Witness in daily life can move into sharing and invitation, and Catholics need concrete examples of how this happens in pluralistic world, where faith may not easily be spoken of. Preachers and retreat directors have to make this kind of outreach real for Catholics: how in everyday life, we have many opportunities to share the Gospel from our personal experience.

The reciprocal side of being sent is the willingness to "go forth." Was not this the initial call to Abraham (Genesis 12:1ff.)? Here basic spirituality demands that we leave, in some way, our comfort zone so we can begin to experience "the other," however that might happen. Going forth has to occur, first, deeply inside us, with a consistent resolution to look beyond ourselves and face outward. **We have no motive to do this, however, unless we feel keenly the spiritual hungers of others, unless we feel a love that impels us to open ourselves to them.** The foundation of going forth is a basic ability to empathize and relate with others, a fundamental posture of concern. At times this may grow into active friendship, at times not. Through the ways we radiate Christ's love to others, in whatever way others can accept that, we are "going forth" by bringing that love to our world.

Parishes go forth in three ways, all spiritually challenging today. They can go out, reaching out to people without faith or whose faith has weakened. They also can be challenged by changes in their neighborhoods, demographic shifts that sometimes challenge the very stability of a parish. Lastly, something that is widely seen throughout the United States, parishes often go forth when they have to merge or cluster with other parishes. The comfort zone that has been established in one parish seems intrinsically disrupted. Unless all these merged or clustered communities see a stronger future ahead of them by engaging others, they will want to stay where they are, afraid and shrinking.

Virtues: Humility and Confidence

When Jesus sends the Twelve out in his name, he uses language that makes us take notice. What does it mean, for example, when he says, "I am sending you like lambs among wolves" (Luke 10:3)? I think he is pushing his disciples to that state most of us feel from time to time when we think we have nothing to lose. Often we witness this in sporting events, when players are so far behind that they throw caution aside and go for broke. Getting to this point means that the game has become more important than anything else. People are willing to give whatever it takes, whatever it costs, with little thought of themselves or their anxieties.

Americans usually do not like low-scoring sports because they involve players mostly being defensive. Our culture likes basketball and football, where numbers can pile up through lots of aggressive action. Soccer, which has low scores and lots of defense, has yet to catch up with basketball, football, or even baseball. Being defensive often means being cautious, not letting others score on us, holding back another's strength. Being defensive means playing as if we have something to lose and we are afraid to risk it.

Playing as if we have nothing to lose involves two key Christian virtues, humility and confidence—or another way to put it, losing self-centeredness and trusting another. To be sent as lambs means we go forth with simplicity, unassuming about ourselves, without undue self-preoccupation, without a fear of looking stupid. As long as we think evangelization is about us and how we look, we can never get to the point of feeling sent and going forth. We stay inside our own little bubble of protection, fearing every move. "Greet no one along the way," Jesus says (Luke 10:4), because he knows we only want to greet people we already know and feel comfortable with. To come to know someone else for the first time takes vulnerability, the willingness to be, in some way, judged by that person. Far easier, we think, just to stay with folks we know. We cannot dispense with humility, defined here as the capacity to drop our non-stop self-absorption. As long as we think it is about us, we haven't developed the perspective that humility asks of us.

Humility, paradoxically, leads to confidence. Jesus expects his disciples to be confident; he must, because he sends them out among the wolves. What kind of sheep moseys up to wolves? Not sheep that fear being attacked and eaten. Rather, the sheep have a sense that nothing can harm them, that they cannot be eaten. Their very lack of self-absorption, their willingness to drop their defensiveness, means that they can approach even what looks fearful. The basis of confidence, of boldness, is not we ourselves. Rather, from the humility that sees God is the central actor in our lives comes an unshakeable sense that God will take care of God's business, and take care of us in the process. This is boldness.

There is, of course, a foolish confidence that appears like cockiness, almost arrogance. Such false confidence arises not from humility but from pride. If such cockiness ever seems to work, this is not because we feel we have nothing to lose, more rashly, we feel nothing makes any real or big difference. "Who cares?" This kind of arrogance ultimately has to fail because, in principle, it does not even see or acknowledge the other person. It sees the other as an object, someone to conquer, someone to fit into one's own scheme of things. People who try to evangelize without attending to the context, to the relationships, to the respect and the tact that approaching another entails, evince this kind of empty confidence. This is not the way Jesus sends us forth.

One of the unfortunate consequences of our Catholic tendency to think in primarily institutional terms is that it can often come across as impersonal and self-serving to people. How easy for us to get absorbed in the parish plant, with all eyes on the things parishes have to show off—stained glass, statues, sanctuary pieces, baptismal fonts, and other such items. Similarly, when we think in terms of the growth of our parish, it may look like we are just amassing influence or money. "All they talk about is money," we hear so often. Our buildings and institutions can substitute for ourselves. As we can become preoccupied with ourselves, so we can become preoccupied with our institutions.

The humility demanded by evangelization might be a way to mitigate this unintended consequence of our institutional side. Just as evangelization is not primarily about us, neither is it primarily about our buildings or institutions. Evangelization, which essentially concerns the Kingdom of God, asks us to shape everything toward God's purposes, both our souls and our brick-and-mortar. Everything, particularly our Church and our church buildings, has meaning in light of the Kingdom of God.

The Kingdom of God

One of the ways to keep perspective (be humble) in evangelization is to have a clear sense of what we are all about. Jesus, of course, gives us that sense. Living for what he lived and died for helps orient our Christian lives. Living for the Kingdom of God, as he did, brings perspective to our lives.

The idea of Kingdom can unfortunately at times be conflated with the notion of "Christendom"—the idea of a Christianity that shapes a whole culture, particularly its structures of influence and status. Perhaps Christian and Catholic images of the Holy Roman Empire best reflect the thrust of Christendom, although such impulses were no less active in the Geneva of John Calvin. Christendom asks: how can Christian ideals come to structure human society itself? One can, when thinking about the Kingdom, unfortunately end up thinking about human society as it unfolds historically touched by the Gospel. Such a conflation of Christendom and the Kingdom, however, misses key points about the Kingdom.

The Kingdom of God is fundamentally about relationship—the relationship that believers have with God and, as a result, the transformed relationships they have with each other. No better introduction to the Kingdom exists than the Sermon on the Mount, sketched by Matthew in chapter 5-7. A disciple's relationship begins with total reliance on God, a trust so deep that poverty, sadness, or persecution cannot shake it. To have this relationship of total trust is already to begin to experience the Kingdom. "Blessed are the poor in spirit; for theirs is the kingdom of heaven" (Matthew 5:3). Jesus has, and embodies perfectly, this relationship himself; this will be verified in the total trust he shows in going to his death.

As a result of this relationship with God, human relationships can also be transformed because believers can now live out of freedom and love. These transformed relationships strive for peace, justice, singleness of heart, righteousness, and mercy. Christians can bring a totally different perspective to human affairs because, in God, they have left behind their greed, anger, pettiness, duplicity, and hardheartedness. In doing this, Christians reflect the end state of human existence when the Kingdom comes to its fullness, as the book of Revelation symbolically represents.

Pope Paul VI and Pope John Paul II, in their writings on evangelization, began their reflections with the Kingdom of God. As God's irruption into history out of sheer grace, the Kingdom is bigger than any one person, movement or era. The Kingdom sweeps through history as it manifests itself in the lives of believers and slowly draws creation toward its goal. If anyone is saved, it is because of their relationship to the Kingdom, even if they are not aware of it. St. Augustine conceived of the Kingdom as The City of God, in some ways opposed to the City of Man; but it is clear that the Kingdom is latent in our experience, revealed in signs that cannot be confined even to the Catholic Church. Catholics see the Church as the core of the Kingdom, but not its full extent. The Church is "sacrament" of the Kingdom, God's definitive sign of divine purposes that encompass human existence.

Is it not evident, then, that evangelization is primarily bringing people to involvement in the Kingdom of God? Evangelization about Jesus and his Spirit means bringing people to the Kingdom for which Jesus lived, and to the Spirit of Jesus, which empowers the Kingdom. We bring people into the Church because, as Catholics, they can live more explicitly and more powerfully for the Kingdom of God. In living for the Kingdom, people become disciples. Through discipleship, they undertake lives that bring the Kingdom into reality.

Evangelization, then, is not about me, or us, just our parish or, in some ways, just our Church. The horizon of all Christian and human life remains ever the Kingdom.

Jesus, immediately after announcing the Kingdom's closeness, undertakes actions to dramatize what it means. His spate of healings, his insistence on mercy, his outreach to the excluded (particularly sinners, "prostitutes and tax collectors"), his challenge to religious leaders who obscured more than revealed the mercy of God, his parables and teaching, and, most of all, his death and resurrection: all unveil for humankind what the Kingdom is all about.

This is why, as a practical and pastoral matter, our Catholic parishes have to be conspicuous with mercy, healing, justice, love, and outreach to the excluded; it is also why we Catholics have to continually review our pastoral practice. Death and resurrection means that from time to time, some entrenched parish patterns have to die. The Pharisees, for the most part devout and very committed people, are brought up so often in the New Testament because they serve as a foil. They show how different Jesus was, particularly when it came to the vastness of divine love. They show, too, how different Jesus' followers must be.

The Spirit, the Breath of Jesus

Death and resurrection cannot happen, insertion into the Kingdom of God cannot come about, without the dynamic power of the Holy Spirit. Evangelization, as Pope Paul VI reminded us, is primarily the work of the Holy Spirit. How can it be otherwise, since every aspect of Christian life is the work of the Spirit of Jesus? We Catholics often explain ourselves only in reference to Jesus Christ. We proudly extol a Christocentrism. We reinforce this Christocentrism with an almost exclusive focus on the Mass. But in truth we reach Jesus Christ only through the gift of his Holy Spirit. Until we speak freely of the Holy Spirit, even as we speak of Jesus Christ, we will be expressing only a part of our Catholic faith and experience.

The New Testament has four major clusters of writing on the Holy Spirit: Paul's writings in Romans 8, John's writings, the writings of Luke-Acts, and Paul's elaboration of the gifts of the Spirit in Galatians and 1 Corinthians. The striking thing about these different traditions is this: they all seem to be based on the lived experience of the first followers of Christ. They felt the Holy Spirit as at least an actual awareness in their lives, both personally and as communities of faith. Modern Pentecostal churches have begun a worldwide movement, with adherents directly experiencing the Spirit in powerful ways; some of this has affected main line churches through various charismatic movements. Perhaps, though, some of the Pentecostal movement has inadvertently obscured the work of the Spirit throughout all Christian life, simply because we can come to feel that other, less overtly dramatic, ways of experiencing the Spirit might be somehow invalid or incomplete.

Pastoral leaders can help open their congregations to the Holy Spirit. Pastors can point out ways that the Spirit is active in what seems like the ordinary lives of believers. To do this, they have to call attention to the dimensions of the Spirit in the congregation's worship and in the spiritual experience, and growth, of each member. Catholic priests, for example, make all kinds of invocations to the Holy Spirit during Mass, but our approach to Mass is often so centered on Christ that we forget the Spirit dimensions of our assemblies. The Mass, after all, begins with the Sign of the Cross, naming all the persons of the Trinity.

Paul, I

Paul's approach to the Holy Spirit in Romans 8 strikes the reader as one long sigh, almost a sigh of relief. Dealing in this letter with differences between Jewish and Gentile Christians, Paul has, in the early chapters, built powerful arguments that both pagans and Jews needed a redeemer. Paul talks about justification as the way God chooses to deal with all humankind because of Jesus Christ, making access to Christ possible for all people. Paul has been trying to show the Christian community in Rome what a difference faith in Christ makes. It makes a difference in terms of the possibilities for humankind (justification, forgiveness, and resurrection); in terms of Christian life (sacraments and victory over sin); and in terms of the frustrations our ideals cause in us. "Who will save me from this mortal body?" he cries near the end of Romans 7.

Romans 8 seems like an answer to that question. We are redeemed through Jesus Christ, who sends his Holy Spirit upon us. "Whoever does not have the Spirit of Christ does not belong to him" (8:9). Resurrection, in this way, becomes a possibility for us since we are in Christ's Spirit, and not living just in the flesh, which leads to death. The first experience that Christians have of the Spirit is their own adoptive status with God; in the Spirit we cry "Abba" ("daddy") to God, showing we are God's children. Christian prayer, following upon the prayer Jesus taught his followers to God his Father, brings an experience of the Spirit and shows us our relationship to God. Next, our experience of suffering shows us the Spirit's presence. No one escapes suffering because all of creation now groans to God for completeness (8:20-21). But when we groan, it is the Spirit of God crying out within us. "In the same way, the Spirit too comes to the aid of our weakness," Paul writes (8:26). So the Spirit is hardly reserved to ecstatic moments of joy or deep emotional moments of consolation; Paul sees the Spirit at work even in our brokenness. This is what fills Paul with so much confidence as he comes to the end of chapter 8: "No, in all these things we conquer overwhelmingly through him who loved us" (8:37).

Paul, II

In 1 Corinthians and Galatians, Paul deals with various manifestations of the Spirit. His issues with the Corinthians all revolve around unity, and the various ways unity was so easily fractured in Corinth. Paul deals extensively with various spiritual gifts (charisms) that members of the community have received—speaking in tongues, interpreting tongues, prophecy, healing, and other acts that seem extraordinary. But Paul, in fact, is attempting to downplay the extraordinary and point to gifts that everyone has in common, notably the gifts of faith, hope, and love. He considers the gift of love the greatest manifestation of the Spirit (1 Corinthians 13) and wishes that all gifts would be directed by the gift of love. When Paul enumerates the gifts, they actually include teaching, helping, and administering, along with speaking in and interpreting tongues (1 Corinthians 12:28-30). Paul's basic point is that the one Spirit bestows a variety of gifts, all of which are to be used in the service of the community and its growth.

In Galatians, the issue is even more fundamental than the unity of the community. The Galatians seemed ready to abandon the teaching of Paul in order to accept Jewish forms, as if their original faith were somehow inauthentic or lacking. Paul's issue here is freedom. The Spirit does not only bestow extraordinary gifts; more basic than this, the Spirit gives believers the freedom to have access to God through Jesus—and not through a set of external Jewish practices that they have adapted. "I want to learn only this from you: did you receive the Spirit from works of the law, or from faith in what you heard?" (Galatians 3:2). Reception of the Holy Spirit in itself verifies our access to God through Jesus Christ.

Paul further points to the Spirit's presence through actions and attitudes that flow from its presence in them and their community. Not speaking of gifts but of "fruits" of the Spirit, Paul enumerates the qualities that should attend the life of believers, quite necessary qualities for Christian life: peace, patience, kindness, generosity, faithfulness, gentleness, self-control. The Spirit, then, abides in the very unity that Christians have with each other. Precisely, nothing must disrupt this unity. "If we live in the Spirit, let us also follow the Spirit. Let us not be conceited, provoking one another, envious of one another" (Galatians 5:25-26).

The gifts and unity of the Spirit allow for mission. Communities in disarray cannot reach beyond themselves. Communities that show the love that God wills for us have the ability to form and send people forth as apostles.

John

In John's work, both in the Gospels and the letters, we do not see the Spirit presented in ecstatic ways. Rather, the Spirit is sent as an Advocate, a Helper, one who accompanies a Christian and gives strength and direction. Although Jesus explicitly gives the Spirit to his followers upon his resurrection from the dead (John 20:22), Jesus' primary references to the Spirit take place before he dies, in the elaborate discourses that John uses as Jesus' farewell message. Here, the Spirit seems to be an agent alongside Jesus, one who continues what Jesus did through the life of his followers. "I will ask the Father, and he will give you another Advocate to be with you always, the Spirit of truth" (John 15:16-17). This Advocate's first role will be to confirm the truth of Jesus. "The Advocate, the holy Spirit that the Father will send in my name—he will teach you everything and remind you of all that [I] told you" (John 15:26). Rather than the Spirit having a separate dimension from Jesus, he works along with Jesus in the lives of Christ's followers. The Advocate can only come because Jesus is raised and departs from them physically: "For if I do not go, the Advocate will not come to you. But if I go, I will send him to you" (John 16:7). When the Spirit comes, however, it is like the wind, invisible except for its action; when it comes, it brings a rebirth, a whole new identity because we begin to see our relationship with God in new ways (John 3:7 ff.).

John's first letter picks up themes of love from the Gospel, and relates them to the community life of the disciples. It is here, in the joint life of the disciples in love, that the Spirit operates and is experienced. In this letter, the community seems to be torn about belief in Jesus; this split has revealed not only a rejection of Jesus as the Son of God, but also a break in the love that should be present (1 John 2:19). This letter seems to refer to the Spirit as the "anointing," wrapped up in the way the community abides in the Father and the Son. "As for you, the anointing that you received from him remains in you, so that you do not need anyone to teach you" (1 John 2:27). The Spirit, then, supports Christ by helping the community affirm the truth of Jesus' relationship with the Father; this truth confirms the unity, and love, of the followers of Jesus. "This is how you can know the Spirit of God: every spirit that acknowledges Jesus Christ come in the flesh belongs to God . . ." (1 John 4:2). The experience of the Spirit, in truth and love, is "how we know that we remain in him and he in us" (1 John 4:13). Spirit, water, and blood all solidify the truth of the followers of Jesus—the unity of their life in Baptism and the Eucharist—which testify to the validity of Christian life (1 John 5:7 ff.).

Luke-Acts

Luke's dramatic presentation of the coming of the Holy Spirit in Acts 2 has to be understood as a connector between the Gospel and the subsequent actions of the followers of Jesus. The Holy Spirit is what allows Jesus' followers to continue his ministry, through deeds and words. The theophanic signs of the coming of the Spirit (noise, wind), the flames like tongues, and the manifestation of language are all symbolic ways for Luke to set the stage for apostolic leaders like Peter, Paul, Stephen, and Phillip. The wind represents, directly, the Spirit, which can be compared to wind (John 3:8) and which links with the root meaning of Spirit: breath. The tongues of fire symbolically represent the powerful preaching of the followers of Jesus, now proclaimed out in the world to Jews and Gentiles. The hearing of the languages represents the growth of the early Christians through many different language groups, all confessing one Jesus and one faith.

Luke, then, shapes the work of the Spirit fundamentally in terms of the apostolic efforts of the followers of Jesus. The Spirit is given so the followers can do his deeds (pray, preach, console, teach), leading to the growth of the Church beyond its original Jewish confines into new, unexplored Gentile areas. Even persecution leads to growth in the Church. The Spirit leads the Apostles to empower Gentile deacons (Acts 6:1-7), to reach to Samaria and even to African spheres (Acts 8); the Spirit empowers the move into the Roman world proper (Acts 16:11 ff.), which serves as the climax of the book of Acts. The Spirit directs the apostolic efforts of the first followers of Jesus, even keeping Paul from going in one direction so, in a dream, he can be led to Macedonia (Acts 16:7-10), to a continent of Gentiles waiting to hear the Gospel.

Orienting our Catholic people to the Holy Spirit means, first of all, helping them acknowledge the Spirit's presence in the various cycles of their prayer, the Spirit actually bringing forth prayer in personal life, and the Spirit uniting and sanctifying the congregation through the action of the Mass (and other sacraments). Pastoral leaders need to help Catholics grasp this more clearly by alluding to the various ways the Spirit is active in the normal course of pastoral life, and by invoking the Holy Spirit as a usual part of our public and private prayer.

Secondly, the Holy Spirit produces an array of gifts in believers, and they often need help in seeing and discerning these gifts. Paul's experience at Corinth can prove quite cautionary. If he had to deal with such an effusion of activity in his rather structured ancient society, how much more can our individualist society produce distortions of the Spirit's gifts? Yet this danger cannot prevent Catholic pastoral leaders from acknowledging gifts as the Spirit produces them. Gifts in our congregations that help them begin to touch the lives of others, leading these others to faith, have to be pointed out, stirred up, and encouraged by pastoral leaders today. The only Pauline rule is this: test every spirit to see if it is in accord with Christ, if it builds up the community, and if it contributes to the harmony of the congregation.

Thirdly, the Holy Spirit brings us closer to Christ's truth—the truth of his words, the truth of his relationship with God, and the truth of our need to commit ourselves above all to Jesus. The Spirit makes us agents in the world because the Spirit comes as Advocate, the one pleading for us and strengthening us in our Christian life. The Spirit is verified by the authentic love that emerges among believers, and by the unity that the believers maintain in Christ's love. This is a Spirit that brings about a new self as we realize the relationship we have with God through Jesus.

Lastly, the Spirit brings about apostolic energy, freeing up our voices to proclaim what God has done and driving us from the comfort zones we construct for ourselves. The Spirit brings us to the "other" in whatever form that "other" may emerge, because the Spirit creates a common language among all people. The Spirit will not let our parishes, or our souls, stay within the walls we construct. The Spirit insists that we see its activity and respond to it in whatever way it is shown.

Grace and Glory

Evangelization speaks so powerfully about the action of God in our lives, and the transforming results of those actions, that Catholic spirituality naturally moves into the dimension of grace and glory. Grace is not only the various incentives that come to our minds, calling us to the good and empowering us to act upon that good. Even more, grace represents a divine dimension in which humans, responding in the Spirit, come to exist. This grace fundamentally produces a relationship of friendship and intimacy with God, made all the more powerful in the revelation of Jesus Christ and the coming of his Spirit. Here Catholic spirituality has yoked John's language about "abiding" with Paul's language about being "in Christ," to form a mystical perspective at the base of Catholic existence. This mystical union with God, produced by the Spirit, bringing union with God through Jesus, is reinforced in the personal and communal prayer of Catholics. Some of the classic ideas associated with the Mystical Body of Christ caught this dimension quite cogently.

In addition, as a dimension of grace, there emerge powers (gifts, virtues) that actuate believers and demonstrate this new, mystical state. Faith, hope, and love, the themes of Pope Benedict XVI's encyclicals, actually are the experiences believers have through their relationship with God, the transformations of mind, imagination, and action because of their union with the divine. These gifts have God as "the object," but they also have God as their "subject" because God's dwelling in the believer, through the Spirit, brings about these transformations. The virtues themselves testify to God's presence. To have these powers (virtues) is to inhere in God even in the present life, and to have our lives directed toward God in all levels of our being.

These initial gifts are accompanied by other gifts that empower us in our moral, spiritual and vocational lives. Moral life, then, becomes the *result* of the grace we have received (and not just our efforts in our struggling attempts to be good), the gradual conquest of all that resists God (sin) as we mature in discipleship. Saints like Thomas Aquinas developed a whole perspective on moral theology by elaborating the various virtues that emerge as a result of the Spirit. Today, Catholics need to see a greater coherence between their daily activity and their status as children of God.

Grace leads, of course, to glory, that quality that attends the state of God that God imparts to those who open their hearts to the divine. Glory begins now, with the experience of discipleship, the reception of the Holy Spirit, and our commitment to Christ. Glory, as our received share in God's qualities, emerges more clearly as we grow in our Christian lives. The glory that we experience here, the glory to which we invite people in evangelization, the glory that our liturgies symbolically capture, the glory of our struggles and achievements in Christ: all unfold into the everlasting, which Catholics call heaven, which is creation come to its fullness, which is, of course, the Kingdom of God come to completion.